Listen, Beloved...

By Martha Smock

UNITY BOOKS
Unity Village, Missouri
64065

Listen, Beloved . . .

Do you hear me? I am speaking to you, not in words but in your inmost heart, in the silence of your soul.

I am the Christ in you.

I speak, yet it is not I but the Father who speaks.

I am the Christ in you, the beloved of the Father in you.

Do you hear me? I am speaking to you now.

I am speaking to you of infinite possibilities that are before you, of wonderful powers that are within you.

I am speaking to you of mysteries of the Spirit, of everlasting love, of unending, eternal life.

I am speaking to you of inner reality and an outer realization.

I am speaking to you of greatness and goodness, of dreams fulfilled, of prayers answered, of appreciation of things present, of anticipation of things to come.

Listen, beloved . . . .

I Am Listening . . .

O loving Christ, I am listening, listening with all my being, listening with intensity of concentration.

I hear Your voice within me, strong and sure and clear, saying:

"I am that in you which never falters, never fails. I am that in you which is strong and steady. I am that in you which gives you strength and courage and overcoming power."

I hear you, O loving Christ.

I am renewed in faith.

I am inwardly strengthened.

I am filled with confidence.

I expect good and right outcomes to every situation.

I expect difficulties to melt away.

I expect mountains to move aside.

I do have faith. I do believe that all things are possible.

I can do all things through You.

O loving Christ, I am listening . . . .

CONTENTS

Listen, Beloved...

Your Life Has Purpose and Meaning

HAVE YOU EVER asked yourself, "What is my purpose in life, what is my reason for being?"

When you feel that something is lacking in your life, when you question the meaning and purpose of your life, it is not because you lack something, but because you have something. You are awakening to new understanding; you are stretching forward in your thoughts and faith beyond that which you have heretofore accepted as ends and aims and goals. Something in you whispers, "There is yet more to life, there is yet more in you to be unfolded and expressed." This something is the Christ in you, the God-self of you.

The things which seem so important to you and occupy your attention and fill your days are results, not causes; they are secondary, not first. Often you are so busy with the outer life that you forget this. You are shaken, sometimes, to discover that what you thought to be your purpose, your end and aim of being, is not enough. Even when you reach goals you have set for yourself, you are left restless and dissatisfied.

Saint Augustine said, ''Our hearts are restless until they find repose in Thee.'' We search for meaning and purpose and forget where the search must begin and end—with God.

Your real purpose in life is to discover the Christ in yourself, to know and to experience your oneness with God, to live your life so centered in God that something of glory enters into everything you do. Then the secondary things take on new beauty and everything in your life falls into place. Centered in God, you are at peace; you are filled with joy and a sense of divine destiny, a sense of purpose, a sense of wonder at the constant unfoldment of Truth in your consciousness, at the constant revelation of Truth all about you.

Sometimes when we think or talk about a subject such as our purpose in life or our reason for being, we let our thoughts get heavy and ponderous; we think in terms of aims, ends, goals; and we forget the wonder and joy of every day.

James Dillet Freeman in his book, *Be!,* says: "For this alone all things were made; to be! Life is not to be explained in terms of aims and ends and goals, but only in terms of living. Life has goals and a goal, but its meaning and worth do not depend on this fact. How shall we explain life in terms of ends? There is no end that is not a starting point."

In your search for meanings and purposes, do not lose sight of joy. The joy of being is within you, unquenchable. Joy is the unexpected, often the surprising discovery of anyone who lives close to God, who makes his every thought, his every act, his every breath a prayer to God.

If you have any feeling that your life is without meaning or purpose, ask for light, ask for a revelation of God's presence, ask that Christ come into your consciousness. In the asking you shall find your answer, and in your seeking you shall find not only light, but joy, pure joy that glorifies and transforms your life.

When you feel dissatisfied or restless with yourself or your life, it may be that you have let your time and thought and attention be drawn away from your Source, that you have gotten off center.

When you give time to meditation and prayer every day, you find it easier and easier to keep

God-centered, you find it easier and easier to keep a sense of God's presence and power, you find it easier to have a constant realization of in-dwelling Spirit, which is the prayer without ceasing that permeates your thoughts and gives strength and spiritual foundation to everything you do.

Your life has purpose and meaning. God has need of you; God is working in and through you to will and to do His good will. God is in you as fullness of joy. He loves to be glorified through you, His child. He joys in your joy and delights in your growth toward perfection. All that you need, all that anyone needs, is to say, "God is with me—my life, my joy, my all in all." God is all, and to live and dwell in this realization makes every moment so full of meaning that we cannot put into words the sheer joy of living we feel.

Your purpose is clearly defined and the path before you is light, as you commit your way, your life, your heart, your mind, your all to God.

God Is Your Sure and Certain Guide

AT THE BEGINNING of each day it is well to pray for guidance, to place yourself, your life, your affairs under divine direction. God is at the heart of your being as wisdom and intelligence. He is your unfailing light, your sure and certain guide.

Think about this as you begin your day. Fill your mind with thoughts of God and give thanks that He is with you, that His Spirit goes before you and prepares the way, that He is working in you and through you to lead you into your highest good.

Do not set up mental roadblocks by telling yourself that you do not know or do not understand. Open your mind to light and inspiration, and ask to be shown.

Affirm: *I see. I understand. I think clearly. I act effectively.*

When you do not know how to proceed in some matter, still your thoughts and wait quietly for inner direction. It always comes as you are truly receptive and in a listening frame of mind.

If you have questions to answer, forms to fill out, tests of some kind to cope with, you prepare the way for your success and for the perfect completion of these matters by knowing that the Mind of God is in you and that all you need to know is revealed to you.

Think of your mind as filled with light, as free from fear or anxiety. Wisdom is yours, light is yours, power and ability are yours.

Are you trying to come to a decision in some matter? Do you wish that you could be sure of doing the right thing?

You can make right decisions, you can be sure of doing the right thing as you lean not on your own understanding but on the guiding power of the Spirit within you.

Whenever you think about some matter that is unresolved, affirm in faith: *I am one with the wisdom of God. The guiding power of God's Spirit is now showing me the way and revealing right answers.*

Do not underrate your wisdom, for you have

the Mind of God in you. Do not underrate your ability to make decisions, for you have the light of God in you. Do not underrate your faith, for God's own Spirit in you fills you with faith. Do not underrate your courage and willingness to act on the guidance that comes, for God has given you a fearless, undaunted spirit.

As you handle the affairs of your life, as you make decisions, as you enter into the multiple activities of everyday living, think of yourself as being divinely guided. This will free you from fear and hesitation, this will give you a sense of peace and security. Keep before you always the realization that you are not alone, that God is with you.

There is nothing to fear, for God is with you every step of the way, helping you to make right decisions and to do the right thing.

to Life-Giving Ideas

HOW DO YOU think of yourself? Do you think of yourself as alive, strong, vital, as filled with the ageless, changeless life of God?

To think of yourself in this way can have a tremendous effect on you—on the way you feel, the way you act, the way you enter into life. No one wants to get into limiting ways of thinking, feeling, and acting. Certainly, you do not.

Your mind responds to life-giving ideas; your body responds to life-giving ideas; your whole being takes on new life as you imbue your consciousness with the idea of life—eternal life, ever-renewing life, life that flows ceaselessly from the one fountainhead, God.

Take your stand for life. Take your stand for Truth. Refuse to fall in line with negation.

Refuse to think in terms of age or weakness or ill-health. Hold to the Truth that you are one with the life of God, that His life in you is ever new, ever vital, ever alive.

Believe!

Believe—really believe that you can be healed! Believe—really believe—that others can be healed!

"With God all things are possible." Establish this faith firmly in your mind. With this strong foundation, you will have no fear. You will have faith in the healing power of God, mighty in the midst of you, mighty in the midst of anyone who needs healing. Know that there is no condition beyond His power to heal.

If you need healing, if someone near and dear to you needs healing, take your stand in faith. Affirm: *I can be healed! You can be healed!* Trust the ever-present healing life and love of God to renew, to restore, to adjust, to soothe, to cleanse, to fill every part of the body with ease, to dissolve every obstruction.

All things are possible. You can be healed. Others can be healed. Know this, believe this, affirm this. Expect and accept healing now—for yourself and for those for whom you pray.

Believe!

Your Wonderful Body

There is life, substance, and intelligence in every part of your body. Every nerve, cell, and atom knows its essential purpose and works always to maintain a state of health and harmony in your body.

If a state of ill-health seems to exist, you can help to right it by realizing that the natural condition of your body is that of wholeness and perfection. You can trust the life and intelligence in your body to harmonize and adjust and heal every unnatural condition.

Do not take the responsibility for healing upon yourself, but let God's healing work be done in you. Quit worrying about your health, quit giving undue attention to your ailments, and relax in the realization that there is life, substance, and intelligence in every part of your body. This is a healing treatment that brings results, for health returns when the mind is filled with faith and the heart is filled with peace.

Trust the wonderful capacity of your body to resist disease; trust its capacity to counteract infection; trust the strong life currents flowing through you to bring freedom from pain, to bring ease, rest, release.

Relax and let God heal you.

Affirm: *There is no resistance in me; there is no tension, stress, or strain. I rest in God. I know that He is my life, my strength, my healer.*

The power of God in you upholds and sustains you. Your mind is at peace, your emotions are calmed and harmonized, your body responds to your steady spirit of faith and trust.

Freely flowing, ever-healing, God's life is strong in you. Hold to this thought, repeat it to yourself. Feel and know that it is true. Know that this is true of other persons also. Bless them, knowing that, freely flowing, ever-healing, God's life is strong in them.

The Breath of Life

God "breathed into his nostrils the breath of life; and man became a living being." You are a living soul, brought into being by the very breath of God. Though you may look at your body as physical, as filled with aches and pains and beset by disease, with every breath you draw you are breathing the breath of God, and there is healing for you.

Your body is not physical, but spiritual in essence. Think of it in this way. Bless it with the thought of its spiritual perfection. You will find that your body responds to your spiritual thought. Think of your body as the temple of the living God, and you stir up the healing life within you.

You are more than flesh and blood; you are a living soul. Your body is not physical only, subject to disease; it is in Truth the temple of the living God, holy, pure, and indestructible.

Take a deep breath right now and say to yourself: *I am breathing the breath of God. God is my health; His life fills me now.*

Does Healing Seem Slow in Coming?

Does healing seem slow in coming? Do not despair, do not give up. Even when it does not seem that progress is being made, healing and renewal are taking place; the life of God is doing a mighty healing work. Say with faith and firm conviction for yourself or for another: *Healing and renewal are taking place. Thank You, Father.*

The healing you long for does not come as a result of frantic prayers. It comes naturally and easily, as you let the healing power of God flow in and through you.

Prayer helps you to tune in to the loving, healing, powerful Spirit of God within you. Prayer helps you to feel at one with the everlasting life force within you. Prayer helps you, when you are praying for another, to let go fear or anxiety and to see that one as he truly is, a child of God— filled with the life of God, healed through and through by the power of God.

Whatever the need, whatever the condition, healing and renewal are taking place.

The healing power of God is mighty in the midst of you. Always remember this. This is the power you are to have faith in, this is the power you can trust utterly to renew you, to restore you, to perfect every part of your being—mind, soul, and body.

Do not struggle and strain for healing. Do not be discouraged if results do not come all at once. Rest in the realization that God is mighty in the midst of you, that His healing life fills every cell.

There is no condition that God cannot heal, and God in the midst of you is mighty; keep knowing this. And keep knowing that healing is taking place. A healing work is being done in you right now.

The life that flows through you, that energizes you, that heals you, is the life of God, ceaseless, unchanging, eternal, ever-renewing.

All is well. You are being healed, for God in the midst of you is mighty.

Christ Is Your Life

Christ in you is your life. Christ in you is raising you up.

Think of the miracles of Jesus Christ; think of the power that is in His name; think of the healing power that flowed from Him to make whole those who even touched the hem of His garment.

Think of Jesus' words, "Lo, I am with you always." Know that the same Spirit which healed through Jesus Christ can heal you now. His Spirit is the life at the heart of your being; it is the power that makes all things possible. It is the Truth of your being.

Close your eyes, relax, and think about the Christ life flowing in and through you. Think of your body as alive and alight with divine life. Stretch forth your hands in faith, take up your bed and walk away from belief in limitation, in negation. Rejoice in the Christ life that is yours. Live in this life now. Be healed by this life now.

Christ is your life. In Him you are completely and thoroughly alive.

Blessed Are You

Blessed are you, for you are healed now.
Blessed are your eyes, for they are the eyes of God.

Blessed are your ears, for they are the ears of God.

Blessed are your hands, for they are the hands of God.

Blessed are your feet, for they are the feet of God.

Blessed is your heart, for it beats with the love of God.

Blessed is your body, for it is alive with the life of God.

Blessed is your mind, for it is filled with the intelligence of God.

Blessed is your spirit, for it is quickened by the Spirit of God.

Blessed are you in heart, mind, body, and spirit, for you are one with God's love, life, intelligence, and power.

Blessed are you, for you are healed now.

Your Song of Life

With every beat of your heart, with every breath you draw, you sing a song of life. All the forces of your being, every atom and cell, join in this song of life, like a mighty, heavenly chorus.

You sing a song of life, and there is no discord in you. There is perfect agreement with the good; there is willing acceptance of life; there is healing in mind and body.

You sing a song of life, and there is no fear in you. There is perfect trust; there is absolute reliance on God's healing power at work in you.

You sing a song of life, and you feel strengthened and restored in every part.

You sing a song of life, and you feel enfolded in God's love; you feel blessed, upheld, sustained, and comforted.

You sing a song of life, and life sings its song in you. You go your way rejoicing.

You Can Be a Channel of Healing

It is not easy to stand by when someone near and dear to you is experiencing a serious health challenge. You long to be able to do something to help. At such times you can find peace of mind and assurance in the realization that there is a great healing power upon which you may rely. No matter what the appearance or condition or seriousness of the need, God is the one healing power. He is the healing power in the one for whom you are praying. Upon this you can rely.

Be not dismayed by sickness or ill-health; God will heal. God's healing power is proved again and again by those who stand fast in faith, who refuse to be dismayed by appearances, who declare life and wholeness for themselves and others.

Be not dismayed by what seems to be; do not believe that anything is impossible or incurable with God. Set your faith to work; bring life and power to your prayers by believing in life, by believing in the healing life of God. Overcome your fearful concern with your fervent faith. God can be trusted. God will heal.

There is a marvelous power for healing in every atom and cell of the body. When there seems to be a serious or urgent need for healing, remind yourself of this. No matter what the appearance, God's power is greater. His healing life flows limitlessly and unobstructedly.

Think of anyone who needs healing as actually living in God. Know that in God he lives and moves and has his being. Think of him as filled with God's life-giving Spirit, with God's life-giving power. Know that every atom and cell of his being are alive and aglow with the healing life of Spirit. Affirm and reaffirm your faith in God's healing life. What is impossible with men is possible with God.

You are a tower of strength to others; you are a channel of healing as you pray for them, as you keep your faith strong, your thoughts positive, your heart trusting. Rest in the realization that life is always God's will, and give thanks.

You Are Needed

DO YOU WONDER if you are needed? You are! Do you doubt that you are important? You are! Do you think that no one cares about you? God cares!

Something in you knows and feels and believes that you are needed and important, even though circumstances or conditions or the opinion of some other person have made you doubt it.

No matter how far from ideal your life may seem, the truth is that you are a spiritual being. You are beloved of the Lord; your life has meaning and purpose; you are here to fulfill a divine plan.

When you think of yourself as a spiritual being, as a child of God, you cannot possibly feel that you are unimportant. You are a unique and special creation in God's sight. You may have forgotten this, but it is true. It may be that you need to lift up your thought about yourself, to let go self-depreciation, and to think instead of the wonderful powers and possibilities with which God has endowed you.

Your good came with you into the world; your good awaits you at every turn. Every day there are opportunities for you to use the powers and abilities that God has placed within you.

Say to yourself, *I am God's beloved child, important and needed in His world.* Lift up your thoughts. Quit comparing yourself unfavorably with others and take your stand, sure and confident as a child of God, capable of good.

You are needed; your courage is needed; your faith is needed; your willingness of spirit is needed; your good humor is needed; your intelligence is needed.

God is with you, guiding you and blessing you every moment of the day. His Spirit gives you strength and encourages you.

As you pray for God's light to shine in your mind, for God's love to fill your heart, you will find your prayers answered in wonderful ways. You will be shown how to live more fully; you will see how to expand your life.

The cure for loneliness, for feelings of frustration, for any feeling that life has become stale or meaningless, is to live every day in the realization that you are beloved of the Lord, to live every day with a sense of purpose, to live every day in the presence of God.

You have much to give, and with God's help you can contribute something constructive to life.

You are needed; you are important; you have something to give—right where you are. God's love is with you to sustain you and to support you in all your efforts. You are dear to Him.

Spiritualize Your Prayers

HOW DO YOU PRAY when you are desperately in need of something?

If you are lonely and unhappy, do you pray, "O God, make people be kind to me; send me some friends"?

If you dislike your work or want a different job, do you pray, "O God, lead me to a better job"?

If you are searching for a home, do you pray, "O God, make someone conscious of my need, help me find my right home"?

If you are sick, do you pray, "O God, make me well"?

Such prayers are answered, of course; but there is a way that lifts our prayers from desperate supplication to understanding faith and spiritual realization.

"God is spirit, and those who worship him must worship in spirit and truth."

What does it mean to worship God in spirit and truth? One meaning of it could be to translate our prayers from the language of the material into the language of the spiritual; that is, to turn from concentration on the need to realization of the truth that puts us in tune with God and our good.

Now the spiritual meaning of any desire is the idea it represents.

So if you are lonely and unhappy, in the quietness of your mind and heart think what it is that you really desire.

In spirit and in truth, your desire for friends, for companionship, for happy experiences is your desire for a feeling of oneness with God and with all people. Your desire is for an understanding heart, for freedom from any feeling of inadequacy or inferiority, for confidence in yourself as a child of God, beloved by Him and blessed by Him with all that you need to make your life full, happy, and joyous.

By meditating upon the spiritual meaning of your desire, you are beginning at the beginning, you are working with causes; and the effects—the friends, the companions, the love, the happiness—will follow. They cannot help but follow the inner realization, the inner change that spiritual prayer works.

If you dislike your work and want a different job, open yourself to a realization of what your need is in spirit and in truth.

The spiritual meaning of your desire for a different job could be a desire for a feeling of true achievement, a desire to better serve God and your fellow human beings. It could be the urge in your soul to use more of your talents and abilities, a longing for greater understanding of life and people and work.

When you think through in prayer and silence to the spiritual meaning of your desire, you will be taking a most important step toward having happier, more challenging work. The outer change will follow, it cannot help but follow the change in your own thought. You will find yourself in a better job—right where you are now perhaps, for often through prayer we discover the blessings we have been overlooking. Or it may be that it is right for you to make a definite change. Whatever is needed, by beginning in the within, you make certain and right your procedure in the outer.

If you are searching for a home, translate your prayer into the language of spirit. The spiritual meaning of your desire for a home is a desire for security, for a feeling of peace and comfort; it is basically your soul's desire to be at one with God.

When your desire for a home is thus translated in your times of quietness and meditation, you open the way for the material blessing to come to you. When you think about what your desire truly is, you open your heart and mind and life to a perfect fulfillment of your desire. You will find your perfect home, one suited exactly to your needs and requirements. You cannot help but find it when you pray about it in spirit and in truth.

If you are sick, translate your desire into the language of spirit. The spiritual meaning of your desire for health is a desire for an understanding of the truth about life. It is the desire for harmony in your heart, for comfort and relaxation and freedom from pain in your body. It is your desire for a realization that God is life, that you are one with God's life, that you are created in God's image and likeness, perfect, whole, entire.

Realization of the spiritual truth about health will bring about a healing in your body. It cannot fail to do so, for an inner realization of oneness with God always precedes outer healing.

As surely as you have a desire, you can, in prayer, in meditation, translate your desire into the language of Spirit. You can lift your thoughts above the need and gain a realization of your oneness with God in whom is the fullness of all good. This is the way to answered prayer, and it works!

You Are Strong

THERE ARE some affirmations of Truth that seem fraught with power and strength because the words have been spoken so many times by so many persons with conviction and faith. *I am strong in the Lord and in the power of His might* is such an affirmation.

As you repeat these words to yourself, feel the power that lies behind them; tune in to the consciousness of the power that has been built into them.

To affirm, *I am strong in the Lord and in the power of His might,* brings a feeling of strength that is more than physical strength. You feel strengthened in your emotional nature so that you are poised and calm; you feel strengthened in your spiritual understanding.

No matter how weak or lost you may feel, declare in faith, *I am strong in the Lord and in the power of His might,* and you will feel uplifted and comforted, you will feel God's strength and power flowing through you.

Let this be your prayer:

Strengthen me, Lord, all through this day.

Pour Your healing life through me. Fill me with Your vitalizing power.

Hold me steady, Lord, all through this day.

Keep me poised and calm, serene, undisturbed.

Keep me centered in Your presence; keep me balanced and at peace.

Let my heart beat in rhythm with Your great love and harmony.

Let the pace of my life be a happy, healthy one.

Let Your life-giving energy flow through my veins and arteries.

Strengthen my mind so that I think clearly and effectively.

Inspire me in the work of my hands.

Direct me in the use of my talents and abilities.

Let Your light shine on my pathway.

Make plain my way.

Reveal to me the way of Truth, the way that leads to my highest good.

Fill me with Your life and health and set me free from every limitation.

I live in Your life.

I talk in Your presence.

I am strengthened with Your power.

What Are You Saying to Yourself?

WHAT KIND of conversation do you carry on with yourself? What are you saying to yourself right now?

You may say, "But I don't go around talking to myself!" You may not think that you do, but you are continually telling yourself all kinds of things. These inner conversations are, of course, the thoughts you are thinking, the responses you are making, the attitudes you are accepting and projecting.

If you find your inner conversation with yourself running along negative lines, you have the power to change the subject, to think along different lines. This is where affirmations of Truth are wonderfully helpful. An affirmation of Truth can be like a conversation piece around which your thoughts center. An affirmation says simply and clearly that which is true and gives your thoughts a pattern, as it were, to follow.

You can change your life by changing the way you think and feel. You are doing this day by day, thought by thought, as you watch the kind of conversation you have with yourself, as you answer any tendency to be negative or fearful or depressed with positive, healing, powerful reminders of Truth.

If you are ever tempted to say to yourself about some situation that it looks impossible of solution, turn your thinking around and say to yourself, *I have faith that with God's help there is a way for this situation to be solved for the blessing and benefit of all.* This kind of conversation with yourself will help rid you of worry and anxiety; it will help you release the situation into God's care and know that in ways which may not now be apparent the right solution is being brought to light.

At any time you find yourself thinking in terms of weakness or ill-health, your affirmations of life and healing can be like a bracing conversation. The very cells of your body will listen to and accept ideas of life and strength.

Let everything in you affirm: *I know and believe that the healing, renewing life of God is in me. I am the healthy, free, perfect child of God. The life of God in me is now healing, restoring, and renewing every part. I live in the eternal life of God.*

Sometimes when you think about others, especially those near and dear to you, you may not find it easy to be at peace about them. You may find yourself thinking of their needs; you may find yourself feeling anxious about their well-being; you may find yourself frustrated and unhappy because there seems to be nothing you can do to help a dear one. This is when you need to take a key idea of Truth, an affirmation of Truth, and make it the focal point of your thinking, the focal point of your conversation with yourself.

One of the most helpful realizations you can have about another is simply this: *I behold the Christ in you.* What are you doing when you behold the Christ in another? You are seeing past the appearances, past the personal self, to the Christ in that one. You are seeing him as he truly is, a child of God, a spiritual being.

When you behold the Christ in another, you are declaring your faith in the Spirit of God in him. You may not be able to see how another person is going to solve his problems or how he is going to find the happiness he is seeking, but you can have faith in the Christ in him to guide him, to bring light to his mind, joy to his heart, wisdom to his ways. And if you are concerned about another's health, you can know that Christ in him is healing life, that a healing work is being done in him now.

Do not carry on conversations with yourself that downgrade your worth and ability. Do not think of yourself as lacking in ability, or as inferior to others. Affirm: *I am the all-wise, all-loving, all-conquering child of God. I reign supreme in all the affairs of mind and body.* Certainly a realization like this is a far cry from thoughts of inferiority and unworthiness! But it is the truth! The more you think about and affirm your spiritual nature, the abler you are to express this nature, to be the kind of person you were created to be. God created you in His own image and likeness, and God loves you!

If you ever find yourself feeling down or depressed, you need to speak words of Truth to yourself that will change the trend of your thinking and feeling. Sometimes to think about just one word can be the starting point—a word like *light* or a word like *joy*.

It is not natural for you to be down or depressed. Everything in you responds to thoughts and ideas that lift your thinking, that turn your thoughts away from darkness, that help you, like the Psalmist, to lift up your eyes unto the hills.

"The joy of the Lord uplifts me and strengthens me all day long." An affirmation such as this can be like a theme song in your heart. Or an affirmation such as, *I am poised and centered in the Christ Mind and nothing can disturb the calm peace of my soul,* can be like an undergirding of faith that sustains and strengthens you and keeps you beautifully serene.

Of all the conversations you carry on with yourself, the ones that go over and over the past—that remind you of what you said or did, or failed to do or say, or of what someone else said or did, or failed to do or say—are probably the most destructive.

You do not want to carry along old hurts or grievances; you want to feel that the past is forgiven and forgotten—and in God's sight it is.

If ever you find yourself dwelling on the past or wishing that you might have acted differently in some situation, remind yourself that God sees you as growing and unfolding and learning. Do not hold yourself or anyone else in a thought of unforgiveness. Be willing to release old hurts, to give up the thoughts that have made you feel unworthy.

You may think that you are unable to forgive

the past, but Christ in you is able. Christ in you sets you free. You can find peace in the present through affirming: *Through the forgiving love of Jesus Christ, I am set free from mistakes of the past. I accept forgiveness. I forgive myself and others. I set my face in a new direction.* When you do this, hurts of the past fade into nothingness. You are able to bless and give thanks for all that has gone before, for all that has brought you to the place of understanding where you now are.

What kind of conversation do you carry on with yourself? What are you saying to yourself right now? Make it a good conversation, make it a true conversation, for the kind of ideas you listen to makes all the difference in the kind of person you are, in the kind of experiences you have. It makes a difference in your health, happiness, and well-being.

"Thou dost keep him in perfect peace,
whose mind is stayed on thee."

Keep your mind stayed on God, keep your mind stayed on Truth, thought by thought. Let your inner conversations be as with the Christ, the God-self of you.

Your Every Need Can Be Met

WHAT IS YOUR need? Whatever it is, it can be met through faith in God. This has been proved time and time again, and you can prove it in your own life.

Do you need supply? Do you need a job? Do you need a home, a car? Do you need money to pay your debts?

Formulate your prayers for prosperity and include a thought of thankfulness. God knows your needs before you ask. The reason to make your needs known is not to quicken God's awareness, but rather to quicken your awareness of God's never-failing, all-providing love.

Do not limit your prosperity by thinking of it in terms of salary, social security, pensions, savings, investments.

Do not base your belief in prosperity on things.

Realize that God's good is not limited to one channel, to one avenue, to one source. God's substance is like a sea of good in which you live and move and have your being. There are many, many ways in which this good comes to you; your part is to keep yourself open and receptive to new thoughts and new ways, to keep yourself free from fear or belief in limitation.

If you need money to meet living expenses, affirm that your every need is met by God's all-providing love. New avenues of supply will open to you, new order will appear in your affairs, new wisdom will be given you in handling the money that comes to you.

If you need a home, affirm that your every need is met by God's all-providing love. There is a perfect home for you, and your faith in God will reveal it to you, guide you to it.

If your need is for work or for more success in the work you now have, affirm that your every need is met by God's all-providing love. God is working in and through you to guide you into paths of success and plenty.

The good that is yours from God is already on its way to you. You are ready for it; you are prepared for it. Accept it joyfully and thankfully!

What Do You Long To Accomplish?

If you are not always satisfied with the way you express yourself, this is a sign that you are growing, that you are becoming more aware of the power and capabilities within yourself that you have not yet expressed.

What do you long to do and be? What do you long to accomplish? You would not have these longings and desires if you did not have within you the capability of fulfilling them.

If you think of yourself as limited by age or education or background, you need to let go this kind of thinking and think in terms of your divine self, your God-created self. This is the Christ in you, the self that inspires you with confidence, the self that urges you upward.

You can be a more effective person. You can increase your talents and abilities. Your self-expression is what makes you a unique individual. Only you can express the powers and possibilities that are within you. Rejoice in all that you are and in all that you are capable of becoming.

God is blessing you now. He is freeing you from unhappy thinking and filling you with His Spirit.

God is blessing you now. The way you felt or acted even a moment ago is already forgiven by His love. Right now you can accept His forgiving love and give expression to happy, constructive thoughts and feelings.

God is blessing you now with peace in your heart and mind about yourself, your life, your affairs; He is blessing you with peace about anything that has caused you worry or concern.

God is blessing you now. He understands you better than you understand yourself; He sees you always as you want to be in your true self. When you are tempted to be irritable, God blesses you with poise and patience. When you are tempted to be fearful, God blesses with faith and courage. When you are tempted to feel bewildered, God blesses you with wisdom and understanding. If you seem to lack interest or enthusiasm in living, God blesses you with a new spirit.

God is blessing you now.

If You Need a Job

If you need a job you no doubt are:

Answering ads—

Going to job interviews—

Sending out resumes—

Following any lead that might open up a job to you—

Willing to listen to anything that might help you find a job—

This is all good, but I should like to add some ideas to supplement all such outer efforts. I should like you to think, not in terms of your need of work, but in terms of your inner gifts and powers and abilities.

There is a verse in Proverbs which says:

"A man's gift makes room for him
and brings him before great men."

To the one looking for work—the one just out of school, the one who feels that he can do more than his present job entails, the one who has been laid off a job—there is a right place for you. There is work for you. As you pray to be guided to your right place, it may be that you will find it in progressive steps. If money is needed to pay bills and so on, you may need to take any kind of job you can find. Even if you take a job that does not use your particular skills, abilities, or education, your "gift," what you are, what you have to give will make room for you. Your truly right place will open to you as a result of your doing with a right spirit and a good attitude whatever it is you find to do.

Sometimes persons who have taken stopgap jobs out of necessity have found that such jobs led to their own right place. Sometimes their gift created a new job for them, in the most unlikely of places. Other persons have found that faith in their God-given abilities, and their confidence in the power of God at work in them wherever they found themselves, opened the way to right employment, took them out of the unsuitable job into the place for which they were eminently suited.

Do not limit yourself by believing that there are closed doors to your good. Do not believe that prosperity and success are not for you, that others get all the breaks and advantages. You are endowed with powers and abilities. You have the gift of God's own Spirit within you.

You, yourself may not realize what your real gift is. There are persons who have been so firmly convinced of what they felt was their particular talent that it took job changes and disappointments sometimes to bring them to the place where they found themselves and realized what their real gifts and abilities were.

In looking for work, affirm with faith and conviction that God has need of you and others have need of you. Give thanks that right now the way is opening to employment for you. And give thanks, too, that every experience you pass through adds to your growth and increases your worth and value.

Think of yourself as on the road to success, and do not be discouraged by detours or delays along the way. You are a child of God. You are needed and important. You have something unique to give that no one else can offer. Your gift makes room for you, and your expression of the God powers and abilities within you ensures you your right place, your prosperity, your sense of happy achievement.

Your need for work can be a turning point, a time not only for a new job, but a new attitude, a new outlook. God can open ways where there seems to be no way.

Now is the time to stir up the gift of God within you, to shake off old negative habits of thought and feeling, to face life realistically. Do not envy others; do not daydream; do not expect to get rich quick without effort. Use the abilities you have; make the most of what you have. You can succeed if you realize the power that is within you!

Are You Concerned or Troubled About Another?

ARE YOU CONCERNED about the well-being of some other person? Are you anxious or worried because you do not see how a loved one will be able to meet some situation or work out his problems? Are you fearful because of a loved one's physical or mental condition?

Even though you may not see how another person's needs can be met, lift up your faith and place him in God's care. Free your mind from anxious thoughts; free your heart from fearful feelings. Your greatest prayer for another is the realization that God is within him, a loving presence, a power for good, a moving force that heals and guides and blesses. Feel your oneness with those for whom you pray.

Give thanks now that God is mighty to restore

and to renew, that His presence is a light shining in and through every situation. Give thanks that everyone who comes to your mind is filled with God's light, sustained by His presence, surrounded and enfolded by His love.

If you are concerned because someone you love seems to be getting so little out of life, if your efforts to help him or to draw him out of himself have met with rebuff, you may wonder how you can help such a person, how you can keep from being critical or faultfinding.

You cannot live another person's life for him, but when you see someone who is not finding happiness in the course he is pursuing, you can pray for his light and guidance. In your thoughts and prayers for him, you can hold to the belief that God's Spirit in him is there to reveal the way, to quicken a new spirit in him. As you pray for him in a spirit of love and faith, you will be kept above criticism or faultfinding and you will not be unhappy or resentful because of his actions, or lack of action. You will give your thought and attention to living, growing, and giving as God would have you live, grow, and give, and you will have the assurance that those whom you love will find their own direction and their own light, in ways that God alone can reveal.

As thoughts of those you love, those whom you would bless, come crowding into your mind, know in the silence of prayer that God is with them even as He is with you.

If you have been troubled at heart over the welfare of someone, release your feelings of anxiety and fear. In trust turn to God and say quietly: "This is Your child. You know his every need. You are with him; You are his life, his breath, his strength, his power. I trust Your Spirit in him. He is Your child, and all is well with him."

Know that as you trust all to God, as you place your loved ones in God's care and keeping, the healing they need, the help they need, the faith and strength they need will be given to them. They will find their answer in God's presence in their hearts.

Let this be your prayer:

I trust the Spirit of God in you to direct your steps and to make plain your way.

I place you lovingly in God's care and keeping with the faith that out of His infinite love your every need is supplied.

I see you as God's child: well, whole, and strong, renewed in mind and body.

I trust God's presence to be with you in all

things; I trust His wisdom to guide you. I rejoice in your God-given intelligence and good judgment.

I see you as God sees you, growing and unfolding through every experience. I keep faith in the wonderful capacity in you that enables you to meet life victoriously. God bless you, child of God, in every needed way, this day and every day.

What you personally cannot do to help another person, God, working through you, can do. Your faith, your prayers, your vision of the truth about another can reach him, can call forth the Spirit in him that is all powerful, that is the answer to his every need.

Where there is a need for wisdom, God is there as light, making clear the way.

Where there is a need for courage, God is there as fearlessness and faith.

When there is a need for good judgment, God is there as loving counselor.

When there is a need for protection, God is there as a shield of safety, as a shelter of security.

When there is a need for understanding, God is there as compassion, as tolerance, as love itself.

God knows the needs of your dear ones even before they ask. God is the Spirit in them that never fails them nor forsakes them. You can trust

God's Spirit in them to bless them in every needed way.

Every time you think of others in a spirit of faith, you are praying for them.

Every time you see others as God's children, beloved of Him, you are praying for them.

Every time you rise above fear and anxiety concerning others and place them in God's care and keeping, you are praying for them.

Every time you surround others with your loving thoughts, you are praying for them.

Every time you hold to the idea of healing and refuse to give power to symptoms or negative appearances, you are praying for others.

Every time you give thanks that God is present to heal, you are praying for others.

Sometimes, to all appearances, another does not respond to prayer. But you cannot know how far another person has come in his soul progress, or how great an overcoming another has made. Oftentimes we cannot see this in relation to our own self.

Of this you can be sure: No prayer is ever in vain; no prayer is without results. A blessing accompanies every prayer. The soul may pass through difficult experiences, but always the ultimate healing is part of God's plan. In a way that you may not be able to perceive or understand, life is always the victor. God's life, God's good, is never withheld. Things change, conditions change, but the spiritual truth is unchanging, as God's love is changeless and enduring. In God's sight nothing is impossible.

The ultimate will of God is always life and infinite good.

Remember this as you pray for others.

Please Stand By

You are watching television, perhaps a favorite program, and suddenly the sound disappears, or the picture is distorted or begins to roll. You think that something is wrong with your set and you try to adjust it with no results. Then a voice says: "Please stand by. We are experiencing station difficulties."

Please stand by. There is nothing you can do at your end. The difficulty is only temporary. Everything will soon be functioning smoothly.

You are looking at the life of a dear one, and judging by appearances; everything seems to be out of order, everything seems to be going wrong.

Please stand by. Do not interfere. Do not try to work with the appearances, to change what seems to be wrong. Do not rush in with advice or plans of action.

Please stand by. Stand by in your prayers. Stand by in your faith that difficulties are only temporary; stand by in your faith that all things can be made right. This is how you are needed. This is how you can help.

When someone asks you to pray for him, he is saying in essence: "Please stand by. Be there. Be there as loving, prayerful support. Be there in faith. Be there in love. Please stand by."

When a dear one seems not to know which way to turn, how to meet the demands made upon him, how to handle a heartbreaking situation—please stand by. He wants your support. He needs you to be there. If he seems to have lost his way, please stand by. You cannot find his way for him; he has to find it for himself. But you can help him by standing by, by holding to your faith in him and the Spirit of God in him.

Please stand by. It is not always easy to do this. We are tempted to try to change the picture in our own way, to step in, to try to set things right.

Please stand by. God is there in the situation. God's Spirit is in your dear one. God's light is comforting, God's power is strengthening. Trust

God. Believe in His power to change every unto-
ward situation, to transform the appearance of
negation, to bring forth good.

Please stand by!

Let This Be Your Blessing for Others

*I have faith in you, because I have faith in
God in you.*

*I do not pray for you to be better than you are;
I pray for you to be as good as you are.*

I pray for you to express your true Christ self.

*I do not pray for you to be happy in the way I
think your happiness lies.*

*I pray for you to follow your indwelling light,
which always leads to fulfillment and happiness.*

*I do not pray for you to be free from responsi-
bilities.*

*I pray for you to be free from worry and anx-
iety, to be the fearless, wise, confident, capable
being that you are in Spirit.*

*I do not pray for you to conform to my idea of
success and achievement.*

I pray for you to express and expand your

God-given abilities and talents in your own unique and wonderful way.

I pray for you, knowing that you are beloved of God.

I bless you without reservation.

I love you as God loves you.

Give the Gifts That Only You Can Give

"I have no silver and gold, but I give you what I have"—Acts 3:6.

What do you have to give? What is the gift that others want from you?

Have you ever thought, when shopping for a gift for a friend or relative, I don't know what to buy; I don't know what he needs or wants?

When you think about your dear ones, friends, relatives, what would you give them if you could? You may think that you would give them something they could not afford to buy for themselves. But even if you were able to give such a gift, it could not compare with the spiritual gifts you have to give, the gifts that God gives through you.

69

What are the gifts you have to give to others, the gifts that are remembered and cherished, the gifts that mean the most, that bring a feeling of joy and happiness?

They are the gifts that only you can give. They are the gifts you can share out of the gifts that God has given to you. Think about the gifts that God has given to you and think how you can share these God-given gifts.

Life is God's gift to you.

You can give the gift of life to others!

How can you give the gift of life?

When you think of others in terms of life and healing, when you pray for them, you are giving them a gift of life, you are helping them to awaken to the life of God that is within them. Your own awareness of the healing life of God in which you have your existence makes your prayers effective, makes you a channel of healing.

Is there someone in need of healing? Give your gift of life. Speak words of life and healing. Behold the healing life of God in the one for whom you pray.

You can give the gift of life, you can be a channel through which God's healing power flows. You can give an eternal gift, the gift of life.

Peace is a gift to you.

It is a gift you can share!

The peace you feel in your heart makes you a peacemaker. You can bring the gift of peace to every situation; you can give the gift of peace to any troubled person. You can share of your peace and serenity with those about you. You can give the gift of peace through your loving and harmonious attitudes and actions.

Is there someone you know who needs to find peace of mind, who needs a feeling of serenity? Give that one your gift of peace. Pour out your blessings upon him and see him centered and poised in the peace of God; see the peace of Jesus Christ filling his soul and making things right in his life.

You can give the gift of peace to someone. It is a cherished gift.

God has given you the gift of joy.

You can give it to others!

You can be one whose very presence brings joy. You can be one who makes life brighter and happier for those around you. You have the gift of joy, joy that keeps you strong and sure, joy that fills your heart with song. This joy is a gift you can give to others.

Is someone dear to you sad or downhearted? Pray for him in the realization that there is a

Spirit in him that lifts him up. Rejoice and give thanks that the Spirit in him is a renewing, joy-giving Spirit. Your feeling of inner joy and your joyous attitude make you a giver of joy, a bringer of joy to others.

You can give the gift of joy. It will be a gift long remembered.

You have been given the gift of wisdom.

You can share it!

When others seem to be groping in darkness, when they are seeking guidance and light, how can you give them the gift of wisdom?

You can give the gift of wisdom by knowing the Truth that there is but one Mind, one source of light and guidance, and by having the wisdom to bless others and pray for them in this knowledge.

You give others the gift of wisdom as you behold the light of God shining in them. You give others the gift of wisdom as you trust the all-wise Spirit in them to be their guide and their light. The greatest gift of wisdom you can give to others is the gift of your wise realization that within them is the Source of all they need to understand, to grow, to find right and happy direction.

You can give the gift of wisdom, and someone will call you blessed.

You have been given the gift of courage.

You can share this gift with others!

Can you impart courage to another? Of course you can, even as others have helped you to stand strong and secure. You give others the gift of courage by your own steady, fearless approach to life, by your own sure and certain faith in God as the one presence and the one power. You can give others the gift of courage by believing in them, by knowing that they have the ability to meet life fearlessly, by knowing that they are never alone, that wherever they are, God is.

You give others the gift of courage by praying for them, by placing them in God's care, by encouraging them to believe in themselves and to believe in God and His power ever with them.

You can give the gift of courage. It is an enduring gift.

You have the gift of divine approval.

You can share it!

You can always give your approval, but how can you give divine approval? Divine approval is the approval you give another from the Christ in you.

The Christ in you greets the Christ in others. The Christ in you beholds only the good in others. The Christ in you looks past appearances and sees the perfect child of God. The Christ in you always gives divine approval, for the Christ in you sees only the perfect self of others.

You can give the gift of divine approval and help another to feel free and joyous and secure.

These are but a few of the God-given gifts you have to share with others.

You have a perfect gift to give to someone every day; the gift of your faith, the gift of your understanding, the gift of your prayers. You have a perfect gift to give to those near and dear to you, to those who are passing acquaintances, to anyone whose life touches yours in any way. You have the gift of your power to bless. How your circle of giving widens when you realize this!

The greatest gift that has been given to you is the gift of the Christ Spirit in you. From this Christ Spirit in you, you can give the gift that encompasses all other gifts, the gift that is the ultimate blessing, the ultimate fulfillment. You can give the gift of the Christ love!

God's Law of Justice Cannot Fail

DOES LIFE SEEM unfair to you? Does it seem that others find it easier to have the things they want and need, that others are blessed with good dispositions, with good looks, with splendid abilities?

If you entertain any such thoughts, you need to reestablish yourself in the consciousness of justice. First of all, in thinking such thoughts you are not being just to yourself.

To establish yourself in a thought of justice, think about ideas such as the following:

No one can take my place.
No one can take advantage of me.
No one can withhold my good from me.
I believe in justice.
I expect and receive just and fair treatment.

I meet life with confidence; confidence in God, confidence in myself, confidence in other persons.

It is important to your peace of mind and well-being that you meet life confidently, that you look at people without suspicion or mistrust, that you have faith in the goodness and richness at the heart of things.

Think about God as a just and loving Father. Think about yourself as His own child, needed and wanted in His world. When you believe firmly in the goodness of God and in the goodness of His will for you, you are greater than any thought of injustice. You can look at every situation that seems unfair or unjust with understanding and with peace of mind. You know that nothing can keep your good from you, you know that nothing can interfere with the working of God's divine law. You meet all experiences of your life with serenity and faith, for you know that God's law of justice cannot fail.

Let Go, Let God

THE ANXIOUS, worried individual betrays his lack of trust in God. If you find yourself tense, keyed up, unable to relax, you should make a deliberate and conscious effort to let go and let God take over in your life.

Are you anxious about the outworking of some situation? Let go and let God take over. You find freedom from anxiety as you hold to the realization that God is in charge, that all things are working out in right and perfect ways.

You may have been living under a feeling of great strain and pressure. All heaviness leaves you as you persistently remind yourself that God is in charge of your life, that His power is at work in you and in all that concerns you. Whenever pressure begins to mount up in you, quietly say to yourself: "Relax. Let go." Then affirm: *I am resting in God. I am trusting in God. I am living in God. I am relaxed and at peace. I am free and happy.*

If you have ever tried to drive a car with the brake on, you know what happens. You are blocked in your efforts. Now a person could wear down the resistance of the brake by forcing a car into motion, but how much easier it is just to release the brake!

Sometimes we try to set something into action in our life without releasing the brake. We may for instance, pray for prosperity; yet we may still let the belief in poverty have a firm grasp on our mind. We need to release this belief by simply letting go of it, and then we shall move forward into a new realm of thought that is rich and prosperous.

You may want health and try to force health into expression. The mental or emotional block may be fear, tension, or anxiety. Rather than straining or striving for results in the outer, set the inner self right; release fears and tensions; let go and let God's Spirit carry you forward into life, freedom, and peace.

Let go and let God heal you. There is strength and renewal in the realization that the pure life of God is flowing freely through you, cleansing, healing, and restoring you. Let go and let God's healing work be done in you.

Are you fearful of the future and uncertain as to whether you will have supply for your needs? Let go and let God's unfailing, all-providing love enfold you. There is assurance in the realization that your supply comes from God and that you are never separated from your Source. Have faith in God's loving provision, today and in the days to come.

There is nothing to fear, for the power of God goes before you and prepares the way. You are guided; you are sustained; you are upheld by God's loving Spirit in you, at all times, in all needs, in all situations.

When you feel put upon by others or taken advantage of by them, when you are tempted to make an issue of what seems to you to be mistaken thought or action, when you are tempted to demand that others see things your way or act as you think they should, stop for a minute. Say to yourself, "Relax, and let go." Remind yourself that God is in charge, that nothing is gained by fearfulness, anxiety, fretfulness. Nothing is gained by blaming others or mistrusting others.

Relax, let go. Trust God. Trust His Spirit in you to show you the way. Trust His Spirit in your life to adjust all things, to ease every tension.

Trust His Spirit in others to guide them, to clear away misunderstanding.

You are right to want conditions and circumstances to be in order, to be just, to be balanced. You contribute to harmony, peace, and the right outworking of every situation, as you have the strength, the grace, the willingness to trust God's Spirit in you and in all.

Relax. Let go. Let God.

Christ Is in You

THINK OF THE powerful Spirit that moved and lived through Jesus Christ. Then think of this same Spirit as being in you. The Spirit that was in Jesus Christ was the Spirit of God, and this is the Spirit that gives life to your body. The Spirit that dwells in you, as it did in Jesus, gives power to your words. It is this Spirit in you that is like a dynamo from which power is generated.

Take the idea that the Spirit in you, the Christ Spirit, is dynamic, alive, powerful, a moving force for good in you and your life. When you think about an idea like this, when you affirm words such as, *The dynamic Spirit of Jesus Christ is at work in me,* you are making a connection with spiritual power. You feel new currents of life flowing through you. You feel the living presence of God Himself at work in you.

Through all the days of your life many outward changes have taken place, but the real you has not changed. In time of failure it has not been defeated; in time of accomplishment it has not been inflated. The real self of you knows, and has always known, that you are one with God. The Christ in you has always been aware of depths and heights beyond the surface self.

"Your life is hid with Christ in God." In your innermost self, your divine nature, you have your real identity. Because of this self, beyond and above the self that the world sees and knows, your life is fresh with meaning and purpose. From the living Christ in the midst of you flow waters of healing life. From the radiant Christ in the midst of you shines light that darkness cannot overcome. From the loving Christ in the midst of you come comfort, strength, and peace. From the powerful Christ in the midst of you surges endless energy. Christ is in you. In Him you are alive!

Christ accompanies you on your way.

Christ is the inner light that shines steadily, erasing every shadow of fear and filling your mind and heart with courage and faith.

Christ is the inner wisdom that makes all things clear.

Christ is the inner peace that steadies and calms your heart, giving you strength and tranquillity.

Christ is the inner power that sustains and supports your every undertaking.

Christ is the inner rightness that restores order, that brings harmony where there has been confusion.

Christ is the Director, the Way-Shower, opening up ways where there seems to be no way.

Christ is the inner patience that gives you peace of spirit and nonresistance of attitude when there are delays or disappointment.

Christ is the divine Companion, the loving Presence ever with you.

Christ accompanies you on your journey, every step of the way.

"Your life is hid with Christ in God."

Christ speaks from the depths of your being:

I am the light shining steadily within you.

I am the light of your body. I am the light that glows and shines in every cell.

I am the light that penetrates and permeates and brings healing to every part.

I am the light that dissolves any obstruction to the free flow of God's life in you.

I am the light that soothes away pain.

I am the light that sheds life-giving essence

throughout your body, binding up wounds, renewing and restoring you.

I am the light shining steadily in your mind,
banishing darkness, making all things bright and
clear.

I am the light of your world.

I am the light of your body.

I am the light of your mind.

Let My light shine in you. Let My light heal
you!

There Is Lifting Up

"When they cast thee down, thou shalt say,
'There is lifting up' "—Job 22:29 (A.V.).

If dark thoughts cloud your mind and cast down
your spirit, say to your thoughts, to your feelings, to your emotions, "There is lifting up."
You are not at the mercy of your moods; you
have the power to change your thoughts. There
is lifting up as you choose to turn away from
unhappy, negative thinking, as you choose to
look to the light, to live in the light, to walk in
the light.

If you are cast down by what someone else says or does, if you feel unloved, if you compare yourself unfavorably with others, say to such beliefs, to such feelings, "There is lifting up." You are God's child; you are a spiritual being; you have the Christ Spirit in you.

What are your longings; what are your dreams; what are your desires? Do not give up trying to make them a reality.

Have courage, press forward with confidence. Know that God is within you, that His wisdom is guiding you every step of the way.

If your life seems difficult, know that nothing can defeat God or stand in the way of His good. God is with you and He is more powerful than any problem. His Spirit in you gives you the faith, the courage, the strength you need to rise up, to press forward, to meet life without fear.

There is always a way out of distress; there is always a prosperous and happy path open before you; there is always a door open to you.

You are meant to be alive and enthusiastic. You are meant to press forward eagerly. You are meant to grow and unfold spiritually, as well as to be whole and perfect mentally and physically. You are meant to know that God is in you. You are meant to express the Christ in you.

Christ is the lifting power in you.

Christ is that Spirit in you which knows neither depression nor defeat.

Christ is that Spirit in you which is always radiant, joyous, loving, trusting.

Christ is that in you which is never bound by habit, circumstance, or limitations of any kind.

Christ is that in you which stands free, unfettered, and unbound.

Christ is that in you which is always strong, always an overcomer.

Christ is that in you which is never distressed nor disturbed by conditions around you. Christ is that in you which is never critical and fault-finding of others.

Christ is that in you which is always poised and serene; Christ is that in you which is always loving, understanding, forgiving.

Christ is that in you which keeps you keeping on.

Christ is that in you which inspires you to accept yourself, to believe in yourself, to be your best self.

Something finer, something greater, something higher—this is what Christ in you, your own God-self, always calls on you to be and to express.

"I Am the Resurrection and the Life"

Does the idea of resurrection seem far removed from you? Do you know that you have been through many resurrections? If you have ever made a new beginning, if you have ever been lifted up in heart and mind and spirit, if you have ever affirmed Truth in the face of negation, you have been resurrected.

Jesus did not speak from a human consciousness when He said, "I am the resurrection and the life," but from His Christ self; and He came to teach us that we too have a Christ self. In Colossians we read, "The mystery which hath been hid for ages and generations . . . Christ in you, the hope of glory" (A.V.).

Christ in you is the resurrection and the life. When you say, "I am the resurrection and the life," you are saying: "There is a Spirit in me that is higher than my thoughts, a Spirit that transcends my limitations, a Spirit that knows my heart and mind and soul. There is something in me that is above and beyond the life that I am living at the present moment, something that says: 'You are better than you know. Your life is more than a routine way of living; you are more than an ordinary person, performing ordinary tasks, living in a world where much trouble seems to prevail. You are Spirit; you are continually rising higher; you are overcoming negation. The world that seems to be continually changing is not the real world. The world that is real is the spiritual world, the kingdom that exists already in Spirit, in the spiritual nature of yourself and all people. You are Spirit, living in a spiritual world, governed by spiritual ideas.' ''

We need not wait until the "last day" for resurrection! We are being resurrected now, we are being lifted up now. The purpose of Truth is to help us consciously place our faith on the constructive side, to place our feet on higher ground, to lift up our thoughts and feelings by thinking of ourselves in the light of our true nature.

If you seem down in the depths about anything, begin to affirm: *"I am the resurrection and the life." I rise triumphant out of every trial.* Know that every time you affirm this, you are lifting your thoughts to a higher level. The thing that has seemed to distress or disturb you will no longer have power over you, for your faith will be in the power of Christ in you. There is transforming power in these words, there is resurrecting power in these words. As you affirm them you will feel a new spirit, you will feel an uplift of heart and mind, you will feel a new power filling you and flowing forth from you, because you have made a new contact with the Christ in you, you have come up a little higher in thought and consciousness.

"I am the resurrection and the life." You are rising to new heights of spiritual understanding; you are overcoming the thoughts and the things that have held you in bondage; you are truly triumphant in every trial!

Let Christ Be Formed in You

Let Christ be formed in you.

Let Christ, the perfect life idea, be formed in your body, till every part of you is awake to life, till every part of you shouts for joy and sings a song of life.

Let Christ be formed in you through the thoughts of your mind. Let the character of Christ pervade your thinking. Let the wisdom of Christ lift up your feelings; let the light of Christ shine through your words and acts.

Let Christ be formed in you. Let the perfection

of Christ show forth in all your activities. Let Christ take meaning and purpose in you.

Let Christ be formed in you as perfect love. Let the love of Christ rule your heart; let the love of Christ control your emotions; let the love of Christ keep you in perfect peace. Let Christ show forth through you as love expressed, as forgiveness extended, as joy released.

Let Christ be formed in you so that the perfect idea becomes the living reality.

Accept God's Gifts

LIFE IS a gift to you.

Life, God-life, fills you, flows through you, heals you, renews you, restores you.

Do you know this? Do you believe this?

"I came that they may have life, and have it abundantly."

"The free gift of God is eternal life in Christ Jesus our Lord."

These are not just words, they are the living Truth about you.

You have the gift of life. You are meant to be well, strong, whole, perfect. The gift of life to you is the gift of health.

The gift of life is marked with your name and lovingly given to you.

Accept it!

Peace is a gift to you.

Peace of mind, peace of heart, peace of soul—do you long for such peace?

"The peace of God, which passes all understanding" is possible to you, for you have the gift of peace.

"My peace I give to you; not as the world gives do I give to you."

You have the gift of peace that stills anxiety, the peace that perceives the power of God at work even when your affairs are troubled or confused.

You have the gift of peace that heals your heart of hurts, that keeps you steady and sure despite provocation or inharmonious circumstances.

You have the gift of peace that pervades your being, quiets your emotions, clears your mind of stressful thinking, and maintains in you an inner stillness, an inner serenity, an inner tranquillity.

The gift of peace is marked with your name and lovingly given to you.

Accept it!

Joy is a gift to you.

Joy, enthusiasm, delight in living can be and should be natural to you, for you have the gift of joy.

"These things I have spoken to you, that my

joy may be in you, and that your joy may be full.''

Joy is within you, even in times of grief and sadness.

Joy is there even when you feel least joyful, even when you are depressed or downhearted.

Joy, a steady undercurrent of joy, recharges your spirits, lifts your heart, restores your soul.

The joy of the Lord is your strength and song—the song your heart sings in the night, the song your heart sings because it knows that the darkness is passing, that with each dawn there is a new beginning.

The gift of joy is marked with your name and lovingly given to you.

Accept it!

Wisdom is a gift to you.

Do you wish that you had more understanding, that you were wiser, that you always knew what to say and do?

You have the Mind of Christ; you are one with infinite wisdom.

The wisdom of God within you inspires your thinking, sheds light on your path.

The wisdom of God in you gives you the power of clear thinking, the ability to make right choices and to come to wise decisions.

You have the Mind of Christ. You are the all-wise, all-loving, all-powerful child of God.

Through the Mind of Christ in you, you have the ability to understand and comprehend all things that are necessary to your progress and success in life.

The gift of wisdom is marked with your name, and lovingly given to you.

Accept it!

Courage is a gift to you.

There is nothing to fear, for you are always and forever in the presence of God.

"God did not give us a spirit of timidity but a spirit of power and love and self-control."

When fear would try to hold you back, when doubts assail you, you have but to rekindle the gift of courage within you. Fear is then conquered, doubts disappear.

You find the strength and the fortitude to meet every situation.

You are not afraid to be alone, for you know that God is with you.

You are not afraid of other people, for you know that the love of God makes you one with all people and casts out fear.

You are not afraid of failure, for you know that with God's Spirit in you, you are able to handle whatever is before you, that you are able to meet life confidently and courageously.

The gift of courage is marked with your name and lovingly given to you.

Accept it!

Divine approval is a gift to you.

You are dearly beloved of God, you have His divine approval.

Do you know this? Do you feel this?

It is true.

God loves you with an everlasting love. Always He sees you as His perfect creation.

You may have moments when you feel unloved or unworthy, but always you are loved, always you are worthy in God's sight. Remember this and do not give way to feelings of being unloved or unforgiven.

God sees you as His wonderful child, and this you are.

God sees in you all the powers and capabilities with which He has created you. He sees your heart; He sees the progress you are making, not the floundering or failure along the way.

Divine approval is a gift marked with your name and lovingly given to you.

Accept it!

You are capable of more than you know.

You are greater than you realize.

This is the Truth about you.

Accept it!

You Are Unfettered, Unbound, Triumphant, Glorious, Free

DO YOU FEEL bound by what you have been, bound by the past, bound by your lacks, bound by the picture you have created of yourself in your own mind and in the minds of others?

You can be free! You can be free from feelings of insecurity, from feelings of inferiority. You can be free from moodiness or depression. You can be free from dependence on anything in the outer for satisfaction and peace. You can be free, because this is the way God created you.

The beginning of your freedom lies in your own mind. When you let go limiting and binding thoughts, you find that conditions, persons, or circumstances no longer have power over you.

Do you think of freedom as a far-distant, almost impossible dream? Do you ever say:

"Someday I'll be free to do the things I long to do"; "Someday I'll be free from pressures and responsibilities"; "Someday I'll be free to enjoy life"? Does the freedom you hope for seem to elude you?

The freedom to be, to be all that God created you to be, is yours, not someday but now. Do not put off your freedom by thinking that you can be free only if some condition changes, or if some person changes, or by thinking that you cannot be free till the children are grown or the bills are paid.

If you long to be free, think about the idea of having freedom to *be*. What do you want to be? What do you want to express? What do you envision for yourself and your life? You have freedom to be. You have the power through the Spirit of God in you, to be all that you have longed to be. You have freedom to grow, to unfold, to express the God-qualities within you. You have freedom to live your life effectively.

Something in you knows that you are greater than anything you have yet experienced or expressed. This inner knowing, this feeling of potential greatness, is the Spirit of God in you trying to break through. It is like sunlight that may be temporarily hidden behind clouds; but the clouds cannot take away the light. Nothing can erase or lessen the bright, glorious, wonderful Spirit that is in you.

Realizing that you are essentially a spiritual being, you are able to step forth, to be the self God created you to be.

You are not bound by anything, any person, any situation. You are freer than you think. Step out on this freedom today. Let go the thoughts and beliefs that have kept you in bondage, that have made you fearful of trying. It is not wrong to want freedom to live your life as you see best. God has created you, a spiritual being; He has put His Spirit in you. God has given you perfect freedom to grow and to unfold; He has implanted God-like powers and abilities within you.

"Perfect love casts out fear." God is with you as perfect love. You cannot be afraid in the presence of God; you cannot be doubtful or anxious; you cannot be bound by what you have been in the past; you cannot be limited by what you have thought of yourself or what others have thought of you. Here in this present moment you are free; you are a child of God; you are standing on holy ground.

Lift your thoughts above the limitations of your life. Let them transcend, for the moment at least, all that has seemed to bind you, to stand in your way, all that has frustrated you or made you unhappy.

Meditate on the idea that there is a Spirit in you that is unfettered, unbound, triumphant, splendid, glorious, free. You cannot help but respond to this transcendent vision. You will feel an inner freedom that has nothing to do with circumstances, with conditions, past or present, with what you have thought of yourself, or what others have thought of you.

You gain dominion over your thoughts, over your feelings, over the circumstances and conditions of your life as you hold to the realization that there is a Spirit in you that transcends all things.

The inner freedom you feel will sustain and uphold you as you go about the activities of daily living. You will feel free; you will be free, for you are Spirit: unbound, unlimited, unaffected by circumstances, all-wise, all-loving, all-powerful.

You Have an Inspired Memory

TRUST YOUR inspired memory. Do not disparage it. Do not ever say, "I never could learn anything or remember anything." Do not say, "I can't remember names, I can't remember telephone numbers," and so on. These are little things, but they are part of the habit-forming process of negative thinking, and you do not want any part of this!

Even if you have thought of yourself as having a poor memory, as unable to recall things when you need to, you can change this picture of yourself. There is nothing wrong with your memory. It just needs a chance to show you how good it is, how inspired it is. Change your thought about yourself by holding to this idea: *My mind is always keen, alert, intelligent. I have an inspired memory.*

Do not be tense in trying to remember things, but relax and let go in the realization that your mind is one with Divine Mind. You will find that it becomes easier and easier to recall anything you need to recall.

You have an inspired memory.

You Can Begin Again

YOU HAVE heard it said again and again, but it is still true, vitally true, that always we stand at a point of newness, that always we can begin again.

You need not give way to defeating thoughts such as, it is too late to begin again, that you are too old to learn new ways, or that it is impossible to change old patterns of thought and living.

Is anyone ever too old to change? Is it ever too late to begin again? For every person who gives in to this defeatist attitude there are countless others who have proved the nothingness of time or age or other physical limitations and have risen up in spiritual strength and power, have entered into newness of thought, into newness of life.

Never let yourself fall into negative habits of thought. Never tell yourself, "This is the way I have always been and I cannot change now." Never believe that there are not opportunities for growth and unfoldment ahead of you; never believe that your life cannot be better in every way.

The way to rise above belief in age and time is to think of yourself as a spiritual being: ageless, deathless, eternal. To look at yourself and life from this standpoint is to see yourself and all things from a spiritual level. You are living in eternity right now. You are a part of the divine scheme of things, right now. Always you can change, always you can begin again.

The present moment is the only moment that counts. What has gone before cannot keep you from rising up and claiming your good, from expressing the abilities that God has given you.

If there is anything about which you have said to yourself, "It is too late," put this thought out of your mind. Replace it with the idea of the spiritual power you possess. Replace it with the idea that now is the only time. Replace it with the idea that old thoughts and old conditions are as waters that have passed away. Affirm: *It is never too late. Today is a new day. I can begin again.*

If you have made a mistake in judgment, you can begin again. If some business venture has not worked out, you can begin again. If circumstances have made it impossible for you to continue in the same job, you can begin again. Whenever you come to a place where some good seems at an end, you can begin again.

Where to begin? How to begin? The place to begin is right where you are. Right where you are, you can let go the old. You can release the mistakes, the worries, the unhappiness of yesterday and begin, right now, today, to change the direction of your life.

How to begin? You begin first of all by turning to God in prayer and opening yourself to His light and guidance. What is needed to be done by you will be revealed to you.

What can you do about a situation that seems impossible to change? It may be a situation that involves other persons, and you hesitate to take a stand for fear of hurt feelings. It may be a state of affairs that has persisted for so long that you have come to take it for granted—you think there is nothing you can do now to change it. You can always do something about any situation; there is always a way, there is always some step that you can take to start things moving in a new direction. The important thing to do whenever you feel at a loss in knowing how to make a fresh beginning is to pray for light. God works through you, but you need to be an open and receptive channel for His light, love, wisdom, and power. What you, humanly, are unable to meet, the power of God working through you can meet and overcome. The wisdom of God in you enables you to look past the appearances and see clearly the right steps to take, the right decisions to make, the right ways in which to proceed.

You can begin again. Know this and believe this. As you do so you will find that you are supported and upheld by God's loving presence. He is with you. He is opening new doors to you and revealing new paths to you.

Listen, Beloved . . .

Do Not Wait to Give Thanks

DO YOU LOOK at your life and long for it to be different, to be better? You take an important step toward having the kind of life you long to have by establishing the habit of giving thanks.

Do not wait to give thanks until every prayer is answered. Do not wait to give thanks until things are perfect. Give thanks where you are, in the present set of circumstances, in the conditions in which you find yourself. Give thanks for life; give thanks for this day at hand. Give thanks for the opportunities to grow and learn.

Your attitude of thankfulness lifts you out of any feeling of depression, out of any feeling of loneliness.

Give thanks to God and look at life with a thankful spirit. In your heart say: *Here I am,*

Lord. I open my heart to You. I offer my life to You. I come to You thankfully, joyously. Guide me, bless me, lead me with Your light.

God Gives His Angels Charge Over You

IN TIMES of need, the power of God seems to rush to your rescue. Then, when you need it most, you are aware of the powerful, strengthening love of God upholding and supporting you.

Your God-given powers are the angels that have charge over you, that guard you and keep you from harm.

Your instinctive ability to choose what is right and good for you protects you from disease or disaster.

Your ability to think quickly, to make decisions, to act wisely, is your protection against accident, loss, or any frightening experience.

Your ability to judge righteous judgment protects you from injustice. You are just and fair in all your dealings, and you are dealt with justly and fairly.

Your ability to adjust yourself to circumstances, to keep happy in your heart wherever you are, whomever you are with, protects you from periods of loneliness or unhappiness.

Your ability to express God's love protects you from quarrels or unpleasant or unhappy situations. You give and receive love, and your heart is filled with peace, contentment, and joy.

Wherever you go, however you go—on foot or by car, by airplane, train or bus—you walk with God, you ride with God, you travel with God.

Going to work and back you are safe in God's care; going around the world you are safe in this same presence. In the familiar pattern of everyday living you are surrounded and blessed by His protecting Spirit; in faraway places you still are with God; He is still with you.

In the arms of the Infinite, you are safe and secure. In the arms of the Infinite, your dear ones are safe and secure. As you meet what has to be met, you find that you are guided every step of the way. You find also that you are more than just guided—you are infused with a spirit of strength, and surprisingly, a spirit of joy—joy that is not dependent on events or circumstances, joy that springs from inner spiritual depths.

At the beginning of every day, place yourself in God's care and give thanks for His protecting presence. At the beginning of a journey, place yourself, your plans, all that is involved, all other persons concerned, under the protection of the indwelling Spirit, for "underneath are the everlasting arms."

God is with you, this you know. So there is a happy way prepared for you, a safe way, a successful way.

Be Comforted, Be Strong

WHEN CHANGE comes, leaving you with a feeling of grief and loss, where can you turn, upon what or whom can you rely? God is in your midst. He is there when you need reassurance, there when you need comfort, there when you need strength.

It may seem that nothing can replace the ways you have grown accustomed to, the persons and places you have come to love. But as you move through the experiences of change with faith and confidence in the power of God with you, you will come to see that truly there is no loss. Though outer conditions change, though patterns of life alter, though someone you love may move out of your life, still there is an underlying Spirit that moves in and through all, blessing you, blessing conditions, blessing all persons.

God is saying to you: "Life goes on. You can meet changing conditions, changing circumstances. You have a place; you have something to give. I give you a larger view of life. Life is not a transient thing, but a continuity. Always there is change, but never is there loss. I, your God, do not fail you. There may be much you cannot comprehend, except by faith, but you have faith. I have given you faith. Be comforted, beloved. Be strong. I am with you."

From the depths of your being, you feel faith surging up. From within your heart, you feel great waves of love and peace enfolding you. From beyond your conscious knowing comes the deep awareness that life has continuity and meaning, and that in and through all things, God's perfect purpose of life is fulfilled.

Always God is with you to comfort your heart, to lift you up in spirit, to direct your feet into new paths, to reveal to you new ways in which you can enter into life.

There is no loss. Renewal is taking place, your needs are being met. Your longings are being satisfied by the love of God, which never changes.

All Is Not Lost

It may seem to you that all is lost, that you can never be happy again. But even as you think this, there is that within you which is saying, "Listen, beloved, all is not lost!"

For the moment, life may look dark, but the Christ light in you, the eternal light of Spirit, is clearly shining, even in the darkness. This light makes a way for you. This light goes before you and beckons you on past the darkness into the brightness that is clearer than noonday, into the brightness that lights up your inner world.

If you are going through a time when you feel alone, unloved, unwanted, you may believe that no one cares. But never, never are you alone; never, never are you unloved, unwanted. You are beloved of God. You are always in God's presence. The Spirit of God in you, the Christ, says to your listening heart:

"I am your life. I am your joy. I am your power to be. I am the love that overshadows hurts. I am the love that draws your own to you. I am the love that pours through you as forgiveness and peace and understanding. I am the love that makes all of life good, the love that ensures the perfect unfoldment of good plans and purposes."

When you feel that some other person has disappointed you, let you down, failed you in some way, as you listen to the loving Christ within you, you hear the loving assurance, "I will not fail you nor forsake you." The loving Christ reminds you that love is not limited to a particular person, that you can pour out your love to all, that you can release any feeling that would criticize or condemn, any belief that someone can keep your happiness from you.

You are beloved. You can rise up out of hurt feelings, out of unhappy emotions, out of any sense of loss or disappointment. You can find inner peace; you can find strength of spirit and serenity of soul.

Listen, beloved . . . .

All is not lost! You are ready for love and life. New and joyous experiences await you, right now!

It Is Time for a Change

IF YOU HAVE felt limited in any way, it is time for a change—a change of thought about yourself and your life, a change from any belief in limitation to a belief in the unlimited power of God in you, which awaits expression through you.

If you have felt that life was passing you by, that it was too late to be truly happy, it is time for a change—a change in thinking. It is time to enter into life joyously. It is time to know that it is never too late to be happy; it is never too late to have a fulfilling way of life.

If you have felt unappreciated, unloved, it is time for a change—a change in your way of thinking. Turn away from negative feelings and think instead of God's great love for you. God needs you and has given you your own talents and abilities to use and to share. As you give what you have to give, you draw happy and loving experiences into your life.

It is time for a change; it is always time for a change, for always you are growing in your faith and understanding and changing old viewpoints and ways of looking at life.

All Can Be Changed

Are you perfectly satisfied with your life as it is? Doubtless your answer is no. Paradoxically, this apparently negative answer is really a positive one. Always there is that in you which is stirred by the swiftly moving current of life. Always there is that in you which urges you on to growth and fulfillment.

One must do more than wish for a happier way of life. On all sides we see persons who desire more from life, but who remain disgruntled with their lot and lead embittered, frustrated lives. The difference between them and the person who turns dissatisfaction into a positive, productive attitude of mind lies in the realization on the part of the latter that within him he has the power to reshape his life, to transform his lot. This power is the Spirit of God indwelling, the Christ in us.

When a person comes to the place where he feels that he has reached a dead end in his life, the question that he needs to answer is, "Why is my life as it is?" Others may be able to offer helpful and constructive suggestions, but the real answer to this question can be found only in the silent, secret recesses of the person's own heart and mind and soul.

If we want a fuller, freer, happier life, we should stop and ask ourselves what our attitude toward life is. When we face ourselves in the mirror of Truth, we may see false beliefs and anxious attitudes of mind that we have allowed to gain a foothold in our consciousness. But if the mirror of Truth reveals that which needs to be banished, it also reveals to us the image of that perfect self of us which is waiting to find expression in the glory of the freedom of Spirit.

Even though you may not be able at the present moment to see how things in your life can change, how you can surmount some obstacles in your path, how you can rise above unhappy memories or binding conditions of the past, through the power of God in you, you are able to do all things.

Say to yourself, "All can be changed." Hold to this realization. Rely on God's power. Cooperate with the forces of good by opening yourself to inner wisdom, to inner light, by being willing to follow even the first faint glimmering of faith.

Thought by thought you can change your outlook and your attitude. Thought by thought you can change your life. You are free to think whatever you choose. You can deliberately, consciously choose to think positively and constructively. You need not try to change all your thoughts all at once. You can think only one thought at a time. Thought by thought you can form a new pattern.

If a thought of dejection or defeat comes to mind, you can change that thought by replacing it with a thought of confidence—confidence based on the belief that you are meant for success and fulfillment as a living expression of God. If a thought of fear or hopelessness comes, you can replace it with a thought of courage and strength by thinking of the power of God in you. God is love—that love is in you. God is life—that life is in you. God is strength—that strength is yours to lean upon.

If you are in ill-health, if you are in need of more prosperity, if you are unhappy, troubled in mind, if you are disturbed by inharmonious human relations, you do not have to resign yourself to any such condition because it is God's will. It is our will, not God's will that keeps us from enjoying the best in life. "Not my will, but thine be done" takes on new meaning when we realize the truth that God is good and that His will is only good. "Thy will be done" is in reality a prayer for a healthy body, an alert and active mind, a happy heart, and a life filled with blessings.

In every one of us burns the inextinguishable spark of divinity, the Christ Spirit. This is why every person knows himself to be better than the world knows him to be. And this is the reason for his dissatisfaction with himself and with his mode of living. What every person, whether he is consciously aware of it or not, wants most of all to do is to show forth more of God, to kindle the inner spark into a living light.

Give thanks for the realization that you are not alone, that God is with you, that His love surrounds and enfolds you. Place all things in His care and know that His law of good is at work, transforming and blessing persons, conditions, circumstances. By the power of God's

Spirit in you, you are upheld and strengthened in your efforts to change the direction of your thinking and your life.

Declare Divine Order

IF YOU find that you do not easily remember long affirmations of Truth, there are two words that you can easily remember, two words that can work wonders for you—*divine order.*

When things go wrong, on days when you feel as though you got up on the wrong side of the bed, how needed is this idea of divine order! Before you let yourself sigh and exclaim, "It's just one of those days when everything seems to go wrong," stop right there and silently, firmly, faithfully declare, *"Divine order."* Give thanks that divine order is established in you, in all that you do, in the work of your hands, in your home, in your family.

When you work in the realization that you are under God's law of love, His law of good, that

His divine order is being established in and for you, you find yourself functioning on a new level. Your mind is clearer, your body is stronger, your emotions are calmer, less perturbed.

Divine order is an inner state of mind that finds expression through you.

Do you want order in your home? Then you need to declare divine order. But you cannot stop there. God works through you; order is established through you.

Do you want order in some circumstances or situation, but do not see how you can do anything to establish it? You need to start with an affirmation of divine order, to know that there is a right outworking for the situation or circumstances. Then you need to leave the working out to God. If you are to do something, or to take some step toward the establishment of this order, it will be shown to you.

No matter how complicated or how out of order something appears, hold to your faith and silently declare divine order. As you do this, you will bring a blessing to the situation, and divine order, the right outworking that is for the good of every one and every thing concerned will come forth.

Let divine order be the keynote of your day.

Is something out of harmony? Declare divine order.

Is there a missing or lost article? Declare divine order.

Are there delays or reversals in some project or plan? Declare divine order.

Does there seem to be more to be done than there is time to do it in? Declare divine order.

Are there feelings of misunderstanding and impatience? Declare divine order.

Are there new skills to be learned, new techniques to be mastered, new work to be handled? Declare divine order.

Are there changing conditions? Is this a time of retirement? Declare divine order.

Declare divine order, knowing that it is being established in your mind, body, and affairs through the power of the indwelling Christ.

Someone Is Listening to Your Every Word

WHERE DOES learning begin? Education begin? With the word. As children we learned to use words. Everything has its basis in the word. Most of the time we do not think about this. We take our words for granted. But Jesus said that man would be held accountable for his lightest word, and He said that by our words we would be justified and by our words we would be condemned.

Someone is listening to your every word and responding to it, either for good or ill. Can you guess who it is? It is your very own self.

The kind of words you speak is of utmost importance, and the words you form into affirmations become living words, words of life, words of power. The words you speak can be alive and life-giving.

"In the beginning was the Word, and the Word was with God, and the Word was God."

At times when things seem difficult or something has not worked out as you hoped or planned, you need to go to the beginning, which is to go to God, to turn to that presence and power within you and affirm the outworking of good. Your word, spoken either silently or aloud, is not spoken to change God, not to manipulate some situation or person, but to impress upon your own consciousness the unalterable Truth that there is only one presence and one power in you and in your life—God, the good omnipotent.

In thinking and speaking along positive Truth lines, you build in a consciousness that stands you in good stead. You are not thrown off balance when something occurs. You are not cast down when things seem disappointing. You are not afraid when storms arise. You are centered in good because you are keeping your attention on words that are living and powerful.

Most of us at some time or another need to remind ourselves of the truth that no person or thing can keep our good from us.

Suppose you are working in an office and the person at the next desk to you gets the promotion you feel was due you. Can he take something that is yours? Here is where your word, the word you speak to yourself, is important. You may never breathe a word of how you feel to any other person. On the surface you are serene and smiling. But inwardly what a conversation you may be carrying on! "How unfair!" you may say. "How ungrateful!" "Why does it always happen to me!" And on and on—often far into the night.

It is good to spare others your negative words and reactions, but you have a most receptive audience listening inside, and your body, emotions, and affairs show forth the effect of your negative conversations with yourself.

On the other hand, you can be a light bringer, a Truth bringer to your own inner world, to your thoughts and feelings, to the conscious and subconscious part of you.

"The people that sat in darkness saw a great light, and to them which sat in the region and shadow of death, to them did light spring up" (A.V.).

Who are the people? They are your thought people.

There is power in the spoken word of faith and truth. Don't take your words for granted. Your words are Spirit and they are life, and they do accomplish that whereto they are sent.

Know the Truth

WHEN YOU have a healing need, or when someone near and dear to you has a healing need, you may wonder how to pray for healing.

If I were to say to you, "Know the Truth about healing," would you know what this meant? What does it mean to know the Truth about healing?

The Truth about healing is that it is a right and natural state of the body.

The Truth about healing is that health is God's will for all of us.

The Truth about healing is that it is always possible.

The Truth about healing is that the life of God in all of us is mightier than any appearance, that this life flows through us freely—cleansing, healing, renewing, revitalizing.

The Truth about healing is that just as life is always present so is the Spirit of God always present, the Spirit that lifts us up, the Spirit that fills us with faith, the Spirit that knows and believes all things are possible.

The Truth about healing is that it is possible to you. The Truth about healing is that it is God's will for you.

What is the Truth about supply? Is the Truth about supply the amount of your paycheck, the figures in your bankbook? Is the Truth about supply the fact that you are out of a job, or the fact that you do not have enough money to feed your family and meet your bills?

The Truth about supply is that God is the source of all supply and that you are always one with your source.

The Truth about supply is that it is not limited to a paycheck; it is not limited to the amount in a bankbook; it is not limited by a lack of a job or a lack of funds. Supply is omnipresent; we live in a sea of supply.

The Truth about supply is that it comes to us first in the form of ideas. We find the Truth about supply by opening our minds to divine ideas and then holding ourselves ready and willing to act on the ideas that come to us.

The Truth about your supply is that it is unlimited. Jesus said, "Seek first his kingdom and his righteousness, and all these things shall be yours as well." He also said, "Hitherto you have asked nothing in my name; ask, and you will receive."

When there is a lack, when there is a need, know the Truth about it. Know the Truth that God is your abundant, all-providing resource, that you live in His abundance right now.

What is the Truth about happiness? It may be a fact that you are alone and friendless; it may be a fact that you do not seem to feel close to people, that you do not know how to relate to them. But it is not the Truth about you.

The Truth about you is that you are one with God and one with all humanity, that you have within your heart and mind a great capacity for happiness.

The Truth is that you need not remain unhappy, that you need not remain friendless and alone, that you need not feel estranged from other persons.

The Truth is that you are a beloved child of God, that you are dear to God, that in ways you may not see or understand, you are bound in love with God's other children.

When you know the Truth about yourself,

that you are a wonderful, beloved child of God, you may see that you have been thinking of yourself in ways that are not true in the sight of God. You may have been thinking of other persons in ways that are not true of them as children of God.

The Truth is that you are meant for happiness. When you know this and live with this realization, you will prove this Truth for yourself.

The Truth is that you are needed, important, beloved of God!

You may say that all of this sounds wonderful, but there have been too many unhappy things in the past that have made you the way you are.

You may think you have gone along in the same way for so long a time that you cannot possibly change.

You may think you have made so many mistakes that you can never really find favor with God and others.

You may think you are too old to be vitally alive, that you have waited too long to try to learn new things or to achieve any degree of success.

This may be what you think, but it is not the Truth about you!

The Truth about the past is that it is *the past*. It is gone. It is as waters that have passed away.

The past has no power over the present, except as you give it power in your thought.

The Truth is that it is never too late to begin again.

The Truth is that it is always possible to accept forgiveness and to be free from past mistakes.

There is that in you which knows you can begin again; there is that in you which is ready to let go the past. Everything in you is ready to come alive, to enjoy living, to enjoy health, to enjoy the present moment.

This is the Truth about you.

The Truth about the past is that it has served its purpose. Now you can bless it and let it go. Now you can know the Truth!

The Truth about the future is that it is not to be preferred over today, for the future will be "today" when it arrives.

The Truth about the future is that it will be good and wonderful, even more wonderful than you can possibly envision at this present moment.

The future will be wonderful as you live today and every day aware of and close to the presence of God. There is nothing to fear about future days. Even as you have met all the changing conditions in your life with God's help and with His strength, so will you meet changing circumstances and conditions as they come.

The Truth about the future is that it holds blessings and good for you, that in the days to come God will be with you as He is now. God's Spirit will be with you to guide you, as it is now. God's life will be strong and powerful in you, as it is now. God's love will enfold you and surround you, as it does now.

The Truth about the future is that it will be good. Let it rest there, and give thanks!

You Have a Great Capacity for Love

DO YOU long for love? Do you long to feel more at one with other persons, closer to them.

You would not have such longings or desires if you did not have within you a great capacity for love. Your longing is God's way of telling you that you have yet more of His love to express.

Do not be discouraged by what seems to be a lack of love in your life. Rather, make this an opportunity to release the great gift of love that God has implanted in your heart.

If conditions in your home seem discordant or unhappy, pour out your love on everyone and everything. See God as present in your home and in every member of your family. Love and praise the good in all. Do this in every situation that seems unhappy or unloving and you will bring

God's healing love into expression. You will bless others and you yourself will be a new person, filled with the Christ love.

When you feel that some other person has disappointed you, let you down, failed you, betrayed your trust, try to see God's love at work. Try to see the divine in the human.

To say to yourself, "God's love is present in me and in all persons and all situations," is to reach toward a greater understanding of divine love that blesses but never binds.

Human love may change—God's love is unchanging.

Human love may be possessive—God's love is freeing.

Human love may be jealous—God's love casts out fear.

Human love may disappoint—God's love is sure, abiding.

You want to be willing to give other persons greater freedom to live their own lives. You want a feeling of security and self-assurance. You want your relations with other persons to be strengthened, deepened, and harmonized. They will be, as you center your heart and life in the love of God.

You are beloved of God. Knowing this, you are able to rise above hurt feelings and unhappy emotions, you are able to release any sense of loss or disappointment.

Knowing that you are beloved of God, you find inner peace; you find strength of Spirit; you find serenity of soul.

You are ready for love and life and new and joyous experiences. You have a great capacity for love, for the love of God is in you, the love that makes all of life good, the love that brings happiness, the love that ensures the perfect unfoldment of all that means the satisfaction of your heart's deepest dreams and desires.

The Weight of Unforgiveness, the Cloud of Disapproval, Is Lifted

Do you live with unhappy memories of acts or words that you wish could be recalled? Or, are you perhaps harboring feelings or thoughts of unforgiveness toward some person or even some situation? You cannot be free and happy living under the weight of unforgiveness—unforgiveness of yourself, unforgiveness of others.

How is this weight lifted? How do you become

free and happy and at peace? When you let the love of God fill your heart and mind, you find that you are able to accept forgiveness for yourself, you are able to release self-condemnation, to let the past go.

As you lift your heart to God's love, you are able to pour out forgiveness to all. You no longer hold in mind or memory any feeling of hurt or ill-will toward anyone or anything. Forgiven and forgiving, you step forth into life, ready for new and happy experiences, ready to express the love of God more freely than ever before.

The weight of unforgiveness is lifted.

If you feel under a cloud of disapproval for any reason, the cloud can be lifted by your realization that God loves you, that there is always a way to change conditions and to make a new start in a happier direction.

The situation that has disturbed you, the condition that has caused worry, your concern over how to set things right—these feelings give way to inner peace and a feeling of trust as you put your attention on God and His goodness. When you feel right with God, at one with God, at peace with God, then all the situations in your life feel the effect of this inner attunement. Your trust in God frees you from self-doubt and you find yourself free from doubt of others. You do not think of them as being unfair or lacking in understanding. You do not criticize yourself and you do not expect or receive criticism from others.

The cloud of disapproval is lifted.

Resting in the thought of divine love, you live in the warm and loving atmosphere of approval of God and others.

Your Patience Will Help to Make Things Right

If at any time you feel disturbed about anything, irritated by anyone, critical of yourself or others, say to yourself, "Patience!"

There is power in constructive thinking, and often the repeating of one constructive word helps us to regain control of our thoughts and emotions.

If you are dealing with children, you need to possess and express the utmost patience. Your efforts will be well rewarded by your own happy feeling and by the response on the part of the children.

If your plans are delayed or upset for some reason, say to yourself, "Patience!" As you keep yourself from feeling irritable or impatient, you make the best of delays, you open the way for a smooth outworking of all that concerns you.

If there is some difficult person in your life, in your home, at your work, whenever you think about this person, say to yourself, "Patience!" Your patience will help to make things right.

Partake

Here is a good word to think about if you feel friendless, lonely, or left out of things. Partake!

What does it mean to partake? It means to take part, to share, to give something of yourself. There is always a need for partakers; there is always a place where something more can be added in the way of love, helpfulness, understanding.

Instead of wishing that others would consider you more, instead of wishing to be included in the lives and plans of others, think of what you have to share with others, of what you have to give, of how you may partake more in life.

You may begin in small ways to partake, but you will find it easier and easier as you make the effort, for participation in life is natural to you. You belong. You are a part of the human family. You are bound to others with spiritual bonds of love. You are not separate from others, but you are one with them in God.

You will find that as you reach out to life, life reaches out to you. You are drawn into participation that is rewarding and brings you new happiness.

You are a partaker in life.

You Can Get Along Harmoniously with Others

When someone does or says something that hurts our feelings, it does not help to brood over the matter. We can have peace of mind and spirit only when we rise out of hurt feelings and bless every person and situation. We do not want to carry along with us bitter memories, injured pride, or self-pity. These are negative feelings that cannot produce good and happy results for us or anyone else.

Is there someone in your life who causes you unhappiness, perhaps a member of your family or a co-worker? Do you find it difficult to think of this person kindly, because when you think of him (or her) your thoughts are filled with criticism, hurt, resentment?

If there is even one person with whom you are not at peace, then you have a work to do, and the work begins with you—in your thoughts and feelings, in your reactions. "But," you may say, "I have honestly tried to get along with this person, and it seems that the very times when I have prayed most and have been most determined to be harmonious have been the times when he has tried my patience beyond endurance."

When you grit your teeth and determine to get along with someone, you are inviting difficulty, for you are not as yet really loving and forgiving in your thought about the other person. Rather than try in this way to overcome inharmony, take the idea of forgiveness and let it fill you and work through you to heal your heart, to heal your hurts, to heal any friction or inharmony.

Today, right now, think about this person, but in a different way. Think of him not as you have thought of him, not as he has appeared, but as he is in Truth, a child of God, a spiritual being.

You may not find it easy to like a difficult person, but it is always possible for you to love a child of God. As you think of other persons as spiritual beings, as children of God, as you behold the Christ in them, you are set free from feelings and thoughts that cause unhappiness or resentment.

You can rid yourself of negative feelings by substituting positive ones. No one can hurt your feelings if you refuse to be hurt. You can substitute a thought of love for the thought of hurt; you can make the effort to bless the one who has hurt you.

"As much as in you lieth, be at peace with all men." What is in you that enables you to be at peace with all people? It is the love of God in you. The love of God in you frees you from fear and distrust; the love of God in you wipes out all bitterness, all belief in injustice; the love of God in you pours forth a forgiving spirit upon all.

You will not, you cannot lose patience with anyone when you forgive him, when you see him as a child of God. He will benefit from your forgiveness and blessings—but more than this, how happy and free you will feel in your heart!

That which you feel you cannot forgive, the love of God in you has already forgiven. You may feel that you cannot trust the motives of another person, but the love of God in you has perfect trust in the Christ, the divine self of all persons. What you see as injustice, the love of God in you knows as an appearance that cannot stand before the law of divine justice. What you envy or resent in another, the love of God in you appreciates and blesses, for the love of God makes no comparisons, but rejoices in the good of all.

The side of love and harmony is always God's side. The side of freedom and joy is God's side. You can choose to be on the side of God and so find an inner peace and tranquillity that nothing can disturb.

Put Your Hand Into the Hand of God

"Go out into the darkness and put your hand into the Hand of God. That shall be to you better than light and safer than a known way."

TO ENTER even a new day is to tread the path of the unknown. Sometimes you may feel that it would be easier for you to meet life if things remained the same, if you never had to cope with the new or the unexpected.

But life is growth, and change is part of growth. You really would not have it otherwise; and even when you resist change, something in you is stirred to new faith and rises to meet the challenge of the new demand made upon you.

You have powers and abilities within you that

you have but half used; and you are not completely satisfied, even in the most ideal surroundings, even when the conditions of your life seem most peaceful and serene.

So you can enter each new day with a feeling of thankfulness for all that has gone before and with a welcome in your heart for what is yet to come. You can have faith in the goodness of God, in the love of God, in the power of God; and you can know that in all things He is with you, that He will not fail you nor forsake you.

In Truth there is no time; "a thousand years in thy sight are but as yesterday when it is past" (A.V.). The time for the fulfillment of your prayers is at hand—not next year, or the year after that, but now. You do not need to outline or plan what the days ahead will bring to you. But if there is any overcoming you long to make, if there is any prayer you want fulfilled, give thanks now that the time is at hand for you to step forth and claim your own as God's child.

The future is as yet unknown, the path that seems so clear and straight now may have unexpected turns; the way of life you now accept without question may be changed, but the certainty of God's care and your trust in Him, moment by moment, turns the unknown into the known, prepares you for the turns in the road, fortifies you for change. Through every turning, you are safe and secure in God. Though human lives and affairs may be changed, your steps are taking you forward. With your hand in God's, you shall not fail. With your faith strong in Him, you go forward courageously and confidently.

Meet Disappointment with Faith

How do you meet disappointment? If you have met it with tears or angry protests against the unfairness of persons or situations, you know how unrewarding this way has been. To meet disappointment with faith is to lift up your thoughts to God, to rise up to the place in consciousness where you can say: *There is no disappointment. There is only God, only good. I see God in myself; I see God's good in everyone and everything. I know that all things are working together for good.*

Has some situation failed to work out as you had hoped it would? Do not give way to thoughts of discouragement. Though at the moment you may not understand the reason for delays or apparent setbacks, hold to your faith in

God's law of good at work in your life and in all that concerns you.

Can you not look back on your life and recall how something which seemed a great disappointment at the time turned out to be a blessing in disguise? You can see now that only your lack of understanding at the time kept you from beholding God's good plan at work for you.

The important thing is to keep on keeping on, to keep your faith strong, to keep your expectations high. Place yourself and all that concerns you lovingly in the Father's care and know that right answers, right solutions, perfect results are forthcoming.

Negation has no power; it can have no power over you as you meet all things with faith—faith in God, faith in His power, faith in the sure outworking of His good.

To have faith is to have courage. Faith is courage expressed.

To have faith is to be loving toward all persons, in all human relations. Faith is love in action.

To have faith is to be willing to work, to be willing to give of your time and energy to accomplish that which needs to be done. Faith is the working power of the word.

To have faith is to give—to give of yourself, to give of your talents, of your substance, unstintingly without thought of return. Faith is the gift behind all giving.

To have faith is to welcome the new, to dare to get out of set ways, out of ruts of living and thinking. Faith is the pioneering quality of the mind.

To have faith is to believe in the worth, the goodness, the integrity of others. It is to allow others freedom; it is to be willing to let them go their way, even though it is not your way. Faith is the Christ in you beholding and believing in the Christ in others.

Meet life with faith by looking for and expecting the good, by knowing and believing that God is with you in all things and that with His help you can do whatever is before you to do.

Meet life with faith by having faith in other persons, by seeing them as children of God, by keeping your vision of them high. Meet life with faith by refusing to be discouraged with yourself or others. Meet life with faith by keeping a positive attitude and a constructive outlook.

Meet life with faith by expressing a spirit of confidence and cheerfulness. Meet life with faith by believing that all things can be healed, that every condition can be made right. Meet life with faith by standing firm and poised, by not getting upset or impatient if things do not go exactly as you had hoped or planned.

Meet life with faith by meeting every day with a singing heart, a happy heart. Meet life with faith by remembering to remember that wherever you are, God is.

Stand Still

Is this a time when you have done all that you know to do, when you have put forth the best efforts of which you are presently capable, and yet you seem unable to cope with some situation or to make any headway in the solving of some problem?

Stand still!

But you may say: "I can't stand still! I must do something. I must take some action."

Barging ahead when you are confused or uncertain as to what you should do can be like going through a red light without waiting for the signals to change, without waiting for the go-ahead, the green light.

Stand still! The scene will change. You will be given the green light. Right now you are to stand still, to cease your anxious striving, to let go the feeling that you must work things out alone.

There is help available to you; there is strength for you to call on, for God is with you. His Spirit of wisdom and power is within you.

When you stand still in faith and prayer, you feel relaxed and at peace and you become a receptive channel for the inflow of divine wisdom, divine light, divine energy, divine strength.

Listen, beloved . . . stand still. You do not have to meet anything alone. God is with you and God is working in and through you and all that concerns you.

Stand still and look to God in faith and trust. See His power at work, right now, today.

God Is in Charge

There may be times when you do not see how some situation is to be met. It may be very complicated and involve not only you but others.

This is a time to keep inwardly calm, to hold firmly and steadfastly to the Truth that God is in charge, that there is a way for things to work out, a way that is in order and for the blessing of all concerned.

This is also a time to refrain from criticism, a time to be loving and understanding. Your loving, faith-filled attitude will help you, of course, but it will also help those around you to sense the power and love of God at work. Even one person, holding to loving, positive thoughts and feelings, can be a center of faith through which God's power flows.

Right now, if there is anything about which you have been concerned or troubled, place it in God's care. With God there is always a right and loving way for every situation to be met. Of this you may be sure.

There Are No Closed Doors

DOORS ARE significant symbols. Think of a door. Is the door you see in your mind's eye open or shut? If it is shut, open it. See open doors, not closed ones. The open door is symbolic of an open state of mind, a feeling that life welcomes us. The open door is a symbol of uninterrupted passage from good to good. "Behold, I have set before you an open door, which no one is able to shut."

Think of anything that has seemed to you to be a closed door and affirm: *There are no closed doors. The door to my good is always open.* There are no closed doors to health; there are no closed doors to supply; there are no closed doors to happy human relations; there are no closed doors to forgiveness; there are no closed doors to comfort and peace.

155

There are no closed doors to the one who has faith in God, to the one who believes in himself as a child of God, to the one who has confidence that God's good plans and purposes are at work in him and his life.

If you have thought of anything as a closed door, give thanks now that God opens the way before you. Whatever your need—employment, right housing, more schooling—have faith that with God you can gain the fulfillment of your need.

If you are passing through a time when you feel as though a door to your good has closed, affirm again and again, *If it seems that one door to my good has closed, God will open a new and better one to me.* It may not seem possible that this can be true, but trust God. He will open the way.

Think about the great open door that God and His love and goodness represent. Think of yourself as entering that open door into a new way of life.

Think of your prayers as door openers.

God Is, You Are

God is love.

You are one with love. Love fills your heart and blesses your life.

God is power.

You are one with power. Overcoming power, the power to do and be, is yours.

God is peace.

You are one with peace. Nothing can disturb or upset you. You are calm and serene.

God is strength. You have strength of body, mind, and emotions, strength of soul.

God is life.

You are one with life. You feel the life of God flowing through you, a mighty healing, cleansing, renewing stream.

God is substance.

You are one with substance. From God comes a continuous outpouring of plenty for every need.

God is light.

You are one with light. Light shines in and through you. You see your way clearly.

God is wisdom.

You are one with wisdom. Your mind is illumined. You know what to do and you do it.

God is good.

You are one with God. You are one with all good.

Let This Be Your Prayer

Dear God, I am centered in Your presence and power. Nothing can disturb me or dismay me. In the darkness Your light shines; in the midst of uncertainty, Your light reveals the way.

Dear God, I am centered in Your love. I feel warmed and comforted. Centered in Your love, I look at the world with eyes of love. I express love; I draw loving and happy experiences to myself.

Dear God, I am centered in Your strength. No hurt or unhappiness can stay with me. Centered in Your strength, I am lifted out of sadness. I am set free from fear. Strength fills me and joy overflows me.

Dear God, I am centered in Your life. Every part of my body feels the touch of Your healing life. Centered in Your life, I feel quickened and restored. I feel the infilling of Your changeless, eternal life. I am healed through and through.

All Things Work Together for Good

All things work together for good. This is what you are to remember, to hold to, to believe in.

When life is seen from a surface view, it may seem that there are unrelated incidents, that things occur which have no meaning or purpose, that some situations or experiences could not possibly be for good. But, underneath the uneven appearances of life, underneath the seeming unrelatedness or chaos, is the unifying Spirit of God. This Spirit, flowing in and through you, in and through your life, works for good. This Spirit speaks to you of the eternal, reveals to you the eternal Truth that underlies appearances. This Spirit inspires you, impels you forward, whispering to your heart and mind: "All things work together for good. That which troubles you or disturbs you will assume its right place, its right proportions. It will fit into the pattern of good that is emerging irrevocably, for God is good, and His work is perfect."

You Are a Joyous Journeyer on the Path of Truth

HAVE YOU ever thought of yourself as a joyous journeyer on the path of Truth? To do so makes every day an adventure in living, learning, and growing.

Even as a joyous journeyer on the path of Truth, you may have problems to solve, challenges to meet, limitations to rise above. Every time you use the Truth you know, apply the principles of the Jesus Christ teachings to your daily living, you make progress on your spiritual path.

Whatever your needs or challenges, you have the power and love of Christ with which to meet them. As a joyous journeyer on the path of Truth, you can meet the experiences of your life with faith, with love, with patience, with understanding.

As a joyous journeyer on the path of Truth, you do not walk alone, you do not live unto yourself alone. Others are with you on your journey, and as you share your faith and love with them, you help to make their life-journey a happy one.

Open Your Eyes

Of all the prayers that we make, there is one that always brings forth a response, that always changes us and our life. This is the prayer for understanding, this is the prayer that says, "Lord, I would see, I would understand."

When you are going through a time of confusion, unrest, or doubt, more than anything you want to be able to see some glimmering of light ahead, you want to be able to understand the reason for the things that appear. It is like going through a long tunnel. You would be frightened by the darkness, by the closed-in feeling of a tunnel, were you not sure that there was a way out, that there was light ahead.

In your need there is always a way out, there is always light ahead. You see this, you understand this when you see with the inner eye, the eye of Spirit, the eye of faith.

Beginning with Abram, in the Book of Genesis, the voice of God within man has been telling him to lift up his eyes, to see beyond what seems to be. "The Lord said to Abram . . . 'Lift up your eyes, and look from the place where you are, northward and southward and eastward and westward; for all the land which you see I will give to you.' "

The revelation that came to Abram was not about land alone, it was a revelation of faith. God, the Spirit in him, was saying: "If you have but eyes to see, you will know that right where you are, all good is set before you. At your right hand, at your left, to the east, to the west, to the north, to the south. Lift up your eyes. What you can see is yours. What you have faith in you possess."

God is saying this same thing to you, right now, in the place where you are. Lift up your eyes. Look and see. Behold the good.

In Isaiah we read,
> "The people who walked in darkness
> have seen a great light."

Have you walked in darkness? You, too, will

see a great light as you open your eyes to Truth, as you look past appearances, as you look through the darkness and know that God is with you, that His light is shining in you and through you, and in and through all. The light dawns in you and you say, "I see; I know; I understand; I have faith."

The Psalmist prayed,

"Open my eyes, that I may behold
wondrous things out of thy law."

This can be your prayer also. Rather than pray for wondrous things to happen, for miracles of healing and supply to appear, pray for your eyes to be opened to the already present miracle of God, here with you as healing, as supply, as love, and as all the good that your mind or heart can envision.

"The lamp of the body is the eye: If therefore thine eye be single, thy whole body shall be full of light" (A.V.). Was Jesus talking about the physical eye? Or did He mean the inner eye, the eye of Spirit, the eye of faith?

What does it mean to have a single eye?

When we say a person is single-minded, we mean that he is not diverted or distracted in his attention from that which is important to him. So when you have a single eye, you look to God, you keep your attention, your faith centered in

God. You do not even see negation. It does not exist for you. Only God, only good, is what your faith, your vision, your spiritual eye is focused on.

To keep your eye single means to look to the light—the light that is eternal, the light that lights every one coming into the world. When you keep your eye single, your inner vision is inspired, and your outer vision is clear and strong and perfect also. Your whole body is full of light; it is spiritualized through and through, so that every atom is alive and aglow with healing light. The inner lighting up of your mind and heart and consciousness always shows forth as healing in the body, as renewal, as radiance of countenance.

"The things that are seen are transient, but the things that are unseen are eternal."

"Faith is . . . the conviction of things not seen." With the eye of Spirit, you see the eternal. With the eye of faith, you see God in all. Within you, about you, before you, behind you, beneath you, above you, westward, eastward, northward, southward, you see good—changeless, eternal good.

Your heart is filled with great joy. Like the man, blind from birth, whom Jesus healed, you say, "Though I was blind, now I see."

Let This Be Your Prayer

To live life one day at a time, one step at a time;

To have the strength and the will to keep on keeping on;

To have the wisdom to handle the affairs of your life;

To have the ability to make right and good decisions;

To have the courage to let the past go, to forge ahead resolutely;

To have the grace to meet each experience expectantly, happily;

To have the faith to know there is no loss or separation in God, that in Him you are forever one with those you love;

To have the vision to see the good in all things, the Christ in all persons;

To have an awareness of God's presence, close abiding;

To know that "underneath are the ever-lasting arms," that God will never fail you nor forsake you;

Let this be your prayer.

The Light Is Shining Within You

Do you ever wish that you could turn on some inner light as easily and readily as you can turn on the light when you enter a dark room?

The power that makes light possible in a dark room is always there, but the flip of a switch is needed to bring the light flooding forth.

When you seem to be in darkness about some need or problem, when you cannot see your way clearly, the power that lights up your being, that lights up your way, is in you. Your faith, your prayers, your affirmations of light, like the flip of the switch, bring the flooding of spiritual light into your consciousness.

When you long for light and understanding, be thankful. Your longing reveals spiritual growth. It shows you that you have come to a new place in thought where old ways and old thoughts no longer satisfy.

The longing in you for light and understanding is God's way of saying to you: "You are able to comprehend things you passed over before with unseeing eyes. You are ready to hear Truth where before your mind was closed."

As you turn within in silent prayer, take with you this thought: *Lord, I am ready to receive.*

Pour forth Thy light, fill me with Thy Spirit, illumine me with Thine own Self.

The light is shining within you, the "light which lighteth every man coming into the world." Your readiness, your desire, and your receptive spirit bring you into the pure shining of God's light where you see and understand.

Think of the light of Christ as shining in you and illumining your whole being. Think of the light of Christ as shining forth through you as radiant life, as wisdom and intelligence. Think of the light of Christ as making you aglow with happiness and joy and well-being.

Wherever You Are, God Is

You cannot be separated from the presence of God in mind, body, or spirit. Wherever you are, God is. And where God is, there is sustaining life, there is peace, there is the presence of all-good.

Sometimes you may feel separated from God, but He is always with you, a close abiding presence. No matter whether you are on the

heights or in the depths, His Spirit is with you
still. In moments of great exaltation His Spirit
gives your soul wings. In moments of grief or
despair, His Spirit holds you close and gives you
strength, comfort, and renewal.

God is with you—not somewhere in the sky,
not on some mountaintop, not in some hallowed
shrine. He is with you, your very life and breath.
His eternal Spirit will not leave you. His hand
leads you, His right hand holds you.

Wherever you are, God is.

Be Not Dismayed

There is a divine presence deep within your soul
that nothing can disturb or dismay. In time of
sorrow this Presence makes itself felt as comfort
that strengthens and fortifies your soul. In time
of happiness this Presence makes itself known as
joy that lightens and gladdens your heart.

You may not always be consciously aware of
the presence of God within you, but many times
every day His presence makes itself known to
you. A new idea may come to you to help you ex-

pedite your work; this is God's presence of inspiration. New courage may fill you because of an appreciative word from another; this is God's presence of love. A reluctance to pass on an unkind story or critical remark may fill you; this is God's presence of justice. A clearer vision of life and your purpose in the living of it may come to you; this is God's presence of light and understanding.

Do not be dismayed. God is with you now, your strength, your strong support. He will be with you always. He is the very breath of your being, the power that moves in and through you.

Be not dismayed. Appearances are not final. Beyond them is the Truth of God which is perfect and unchanging. There is no appearance that is more powerful than God; there is no condition that cannot be healed, no situation that cannot be made right.

Be not dismayed. When change comes, God is with you, unchanging. His Spirit has always been with you, will always be with you. He is in the new and the unfamiliar; wherever you are, whatever you do, God is with you.

Be not dismayed. God is life without end. In ways that we do not presently see or understand, His good plans and purposes are being fulfilled.

Let This Be Your Prayer

Keep me serene, O loving Lord. Keep me so aware of Your powerful, guiding Spirit in the midst of me that there is no room in me for doubt or fear or anxiety about anything.

O loving Lord, help me to be sure and steady in my efforts to accomplish the tasks that are before me. Keep me from confused thinking, from any feeling of haste or pressure. As I do all things in the awareness that I am not alone, that I do not depend only on personal efforts or personal power, I am strengthened; I am able to enlarge my scope of activities.

Be with me, Lord, as a loving presence. Inspire me with new vision, reveal the Truth to me in ways that I can understand.

Bless me, O loving Lord, and bless the people in my life so that they, whatever their particular needs or hopes or dreams, may feel Your loving presence and keep serene, steady, poised, and happy, moment by moment, hour by hour.

Now Is the Time

Do not grieve or sorrow over the past. Do not long for the days that are no more. Do not wish that you could go back and relive some experience or change something that cannot be changed. Let the past go by blessing it. Bless all the experiences in your life; bless all the persons who have been part of the changing scene of your life. Bless the good memories and bless the memories that may seem painful to recall. As you bless, you are blessed; as you release, you are released; as you forgive, you are forgiven.

Remember the words, "A garland for ashes, the oil of joy for mourning, the garment of praise for the spirit of heaviness" (A.V.). This means that through God's love, all is transformed, all is changed into something good and beautiful.

Let light into your life; let love into your life; let joy into your life; let a spirit of newness into your life. Bless the past and let it go.

Do not put off your good. Do not just think about how wonderful it would be to live by great ideas, to stand by great principles. Begin to do it, now, today!

Do not say that if only you had known about

Truth teachings sooner, your life would be different. Begin, now, today to follow through on the understanding you have, to live the Truth you know.

Now is the time. Now is the time to prove God's power in your life. Now is the time to set your faith into action. Now is the time to be fearless and free. Now is the time to be healthy and whole. Now is the time to be successful and prosperous. Now is the time to feel wonderfully blessed and marvelously sustained, for now are you God's child, now are you filled with His life, now are you one with His love. Now are you triumphant in your overcoming.

This is the moment to work with; where you are now is the place to begin. It may seem that you are in a waiting period in your life, that you cannot really live the kind of life you should like to live until circumstances change, until you have some opportunity that you feel has been denied you, until you are set free from bondage to some condition, or perhaps some person. But there is really no other time than the present. You need to use what you have where you are; you need to put forth the effort that is needed now to make your life more receptive to good, to make you a producer of good.

Today is important. It is a day in which you

can learn and grow, in which you can give and gain. Enter into the joy of the present; let the past go; take your eyes off the distant fields of the future. Now is the time. Now are you alive in God. Now are you needed in His world. Now is good brought forth into the world in new and wondrous ways through you.

Listen, Beloved . . .

to What You Are—

YOU ARE wonderfully and intricately made. Your body, which you may take for granted, or may despair of because of its aches and pains and failings, is a holy creation—it is the temple of the living God. Its trillions of atoms and cells are composed of life itself. You are alive with the life of God. If you need healing, the capacity for healing is there, right within you. God who created you, dwells within you. He is always present to heal.

You are the very life of God in expression. You are one with eternal, unending life. You were created perfect; you are meant for perfection. You are a living miracle!

Listen, beloved, to what you are—

You are a child of God. You are the Christ of

God in expression in the world. In your Christ self you are triumphant, victorious, free. Nothing can hurt you, upset you, or make you afraid. As God's child, as the Christ of God that you are, you rise up out of any limitation, you are not downed by any circumstance. You are not defeated by setbacks or failures. You have the infinite capacity to hold fast, to persevere, to refuse to be discouraged or disheartened.

In all of life's experiences, you feel the strong, loving support of God's presence. You know that you are not alone, that you do not have to meet anything alone. God is with you. In times of great joy, God is there. In times when you feel rejected or unworthy, God is there. As you listen to the inner voice, your heart hears only assurances of love. God says in your secret heart: "You are my child. I love you. I have faith in you." The discouragement, the bitterness, the feeling of despair, the tears—all give way, all are as nothing.

God loves you. He sees you as His spiritual creation. He sees what you are and what you are becoming.

Listen, beloved, to what you are—

You are wonderful, remarkable, lovable, unique! You are a spiritual being, now and forever. You are needed and important. You have depths you have never plumbed, heights you have never soared. You have greatness of spirit. You have inner strength and power. You have a glorious capacity for living and loving and giving.

Listen, beloved, to what you are—

It is the Truth about you!

Printed in the United States of America   148-F-4375-20M-9-80